DISCARD

Current
CONTROVERSIES

Drug Legalization

Other Books in the Current Controversies Series

Drug Legalization

Noël Merino, Book Editor

GREENHAVEN PRESS
A part of Gale, Cengage Learning

Farmington Hills, Mich • San Francisco • New York • Waterville, Maine
Meriden, Conn • Mason, Ohio • Chicago

Patricia Coryell, *Vice President & Publisher, New Products & GVRL*
Douglas Dentino, *Manager, New Products*
Judy Galens, *Acquisitions Editor*

For more information, contact:
Greenhaven Press
27500 Drake Rd.
Farmington Hills, MI 48331-3535
Or you can visit our Internet site at gale.cengage.com

Articles in Greenhaven Press anthologies are often edited for length to meet page requirements. In addition, original titles of these works are changed to clearly present the main thesis and to explicitly indicate the author's opinion. Every effort is made to ensure that Greenhaven Press accurately reflects the original intent of the authors. Every effort has been made to trace the owners of copyrighted material.

Cover image copyright © william casey/Shutterstock.com.

LIBRARY OF CONGRESS CATALOGING-IN-PUBLICATION DATA

Drug legalization / Noël Merino, book editor.
    pages cm. -- (Current controversies)
Includes bibliographical references and index.
    ISBN 978-0-7377-7215-9 (hardback) -- ISBN 978-0-7377-7216-6 (paperback)
    1. Drug legalization--United States--Juvenile literature. 2. Drug control--United States--Juvenile literature. I. Merino, Noël.
    HV5825.D77667 2015
    363.450973--dc23
                                                                    2014034674

Contents

Chapter 2: Is Drug Use Dangerous for Society?

Ideally, marijuana use and possession should be legalized; but if that is not possible, use and possession should be depenalized or, at minimum, decriminalized. Legalizing or depenalizing marijuana is the best way to eliminate the disparity in arrests between people of color and whites for possession of marijuana.

No: Marijuana Should Not Be Legalized

Chapter 4: How Should US Drug Policy Be Reformed?

Legalization of heroin and other hard drugs is very different than legalization of marijuana and would result in far worse costs to society. While the so-called war on drugs has been a failure, we should think carefully before we legalize highly addictive drugs like heroine.

The US government's prohibition of drugs violates foundational rights of our democracy, specifically the right to pursue happiness and the right of self-ownership. The human cost of the war on drugs is also immoral, and for these reasons it should be ended.

Although public support for drug legalization is on the rise, in light of the failures of prohibition, there are potential negatives to legalization that need to be acknowledged before such changes occur.

Foreword

By definition, controversies are "discussions of questions in which opposing opinions clash" (Webster's Twentieth Century Dictionary Unabridged). Few would deny that controversies are a pervasive part of the human condition and exist on virtually every level of human enterprise. Controversies transpire between individuals and among groups, within nations and between nations. Controversies supply the grist necessary for progress by providing challenges and challengers to the status quo. They also create atmospheres where strife and warfare can flourish. A world without controversies would be a peaceful world; but it also would be, by and large, static and prosaic.

The Series' Purpose

The purpose of the Current Controversies series is to explore many of the social, political, and economic controversies dominating the national and international scenes today. Titles selected for inclusion in the series are highly focused and specific. For example, from the larger category of criminal justice, Current Controversies deals with specific topics such as police brutality, gun control, white collar crime, and others. The debates in Current Controversies also are presented in a useful, timeless fashion. Articles and book excerpts included in each title are selected if they contribute valuable, long-range ideas to the overall debate. And wherever possible, current information is enhanced with historical documents and other relevant materials. Thus, while individual titles are current in focus, every effort is made to ensure that they will not become quickly outdated. Books in the Current Controversies series will remain important resources for librarians, teachers, and students for many years.

In addition to keeping the titles focused and specific, great care is taken in the editorial format of each book in the series. Book introductions and chapter prefaces are offered to provide background material for readers. Chapters are organized around several key questions that are answered with diverse opinions representing all points on the political spectrum. Materials in each chapter include opinions in which authors clearly disagree as well as alternative opinions in which authors may agree on a broader issue but disagree on the possible solutions. In this way, the content of each volume in Current Controversies mirrors the mosaic of opinions encountered in society. Readers will quickly realize that there are many viable answers to these complex issues. By questioning each author's conclusions, students and casual readers can begin to develop the critical thinking skills so important to evaluating opinionated material.

Current Controversies is also ideal for controlled research. Each anthology in the series is composed of primary sources taken from a wide gamut of informational categories including periodicals, newspapers, books, US and foreign government documents, and the publications of private and public organizations. Readers will find factual support for reports, debates, and research papers covering all areas of important issues. In addition, an annotated table of contents, an index, a book and periodical bibliography, and a list of organizations to contact are included in each book to expedite further research.

Perhaps more than ever before in history, people are confronted with diverse and contradictory information. During the Persian Gulf War, for example, the public was not only treated to minute-to-minute coverage of the war, it was also inundated with critiques of the coverage and countless analyses of the factors motivating US involvement. Being able to sort through the plethora of opinions accompanying today's major issues, and to draw one's own conclusions, can be a complicated and frustrating struggle. It is the editors' hope that Current Controversies will help readers with this struggle.

Introduction

"A 2014 Pew Research poll found that two-thirds of Americans favor providing treatment to those who use illegal drugs rather than prosecuting them criminally."

In 1971, then US president Richard Nixon launched a new era of drug policy in the country. In a speech at the White House he said, "America's public enemy number one in the United States is drug abuse. In order to fight and defeat this enemy, it is necessary to wage a new, all-out offensive." Thus began the War on Drugs. In 1973, the Drug Enforcement Administration (DEA) was created with an annual budget of under $75 million. More than forty years later that budget has increased to over $2 billion.

The Controlled Substances Act (CSA) was passed as part of the Comprehensive Drug Abuse Prevention and Control Act of 1970. The CSA categorizes drugs according to perceived risk of abuse and accepted medical uses, making the manufacture, distribution, and possession of certain substances subject to federal regulation. Drugs such as heroin and marijuana have been classified by the federal government as having a high risk of abuse and no legitimate medical use and, as such, prohibited in all circumstances. Other drugs considered as having a risk of abuse or dependence but also with accepted medical uses are available only from a physician. Drugs in this category include cocaine and various prescription drugs.

Federal law regulates the criminal penalties that may be imposed for a conviction of a violation of the CSA. Penalties for drug trafficking at the federal level—trafficking across state lines, from outside the United States, or within the District of Columbia—depend on the quantity of drugs possessed, and sentences vary from a fine to life imprisonment. Penalties for simple possession at the federal level range from a fine to three years imprisonment. However, there are mandatory minimum sentences for certain amounts and for repeat offenders. In addition to federal laws, states have their own laws regulating the criminal penalties for the manufacture, distribution, and possession of illegal drugs.

The justification most often given for the prohibition of certain drugs is to protect the drug user and society from harm. Addiction, health risks, crime, and lowered productivity are among the many alleged harms that are said to justify the prohibition on certain drugs. Proponents of prohibition argue that criminalization is the best way to deter drug production and use, thereby minimizing the potential harms of drugs to society.

Proponents of drug legalization argue that the current prohibition on the manufacture, distribution, and possession of certain drugs should end. Calls for drug legalization rarely propose a complete absence of government regulation. Rather, calls for legalization frequently argue that legal drugs be treated like alcohol and tobacco, with restrictions on the manufacture of the substances, the age of legal use, the place of sale, and the use of automobiles and machinery under the influence. Additionally, proponents of drug legalization do not always want all drugs treated the same: a majority of Americans favor the legalization of marijuana, but only a small minority support the legalization of cocaine, heroin, and methamphetamine.

One of the nuanced distinctions in the drug legalization debate is between legalization and decriminalization. Drug decriminalization calls for eliminating the criminal penalties placed upon drug use (although not usually for drug production), without complete legal sanctioning. Proponents of drug decriminalization stop short of calling for drugs to be regulated by the government—such as alcohol and tobacco are—but propose that prison sentences and criminal records for drug use end. Proponents of decriminalization contend that society suffers many harms from prohibition, such as increased violence and the costs of incarcerating drug users, which could be reduced by a policy of decriminalization.

The debate over drug legalization in the United States has reached a tipping point in recent years: a 2014 Pew Research poll found that two-thirds of Americans favor providing treatment to those who use illegal drugs rather than prosecuting them criminally. Approximately half of the states have legalized marijuana for medical use and two states—Colorado and Washington—have legalized recreational marijuana use for adults aged twenty-one and older. In addition, many cities have adopted relaxed policies toward individual marijuana possession for recreational use. Whether these recent changes in marijuana policy constitute a nationwide trend and whether such policies will eventually be extended to other drugs remains to be seen. The current debates about drug legalization are explored in *Current Controversies: Drug Legalization*, shedding light on this fascinating and complicated issue.

Is the Prohibition of Drugs Failing?

Overview: Is the War on Drugs Nearing an End?

Matt Sledge

Matt Sledge is a reporter for The Huffington Post.

For four decades, libertarians, civil rights activists and drug treatment experts have stood outside of the political mainstream in arguing that the war on drugs was sending too many people to prison, wasting too much money, wrenching apart too many families—and all for little or no public benefit.

They were always in the minority. But on Thursday, a sign of a new reality emerged: for the first time in four decades of polling, the Pew Research Center found that more than half of Americans support legalizing marijuana.

That finding is the result of decades of slow demographic changes and cultural evolution that now appears, much like attitudes around marriage equality, to be accelerating. More and more people, including Pat Robertson and Sen. Rand Paul (R-Ky), are rejecting the tough-on-crime rhetoric so long directed toward drug use.

But in its latest budget, the White House still requested $25.6 billion to combat drug use just at the federal level, with well more than half of that going toward a strategy centered around law enforcement. The drug war has helped swell America's prison and jail population to 2.2 million people—meaning that a country with five percent of the world's population contains one quarter of its prisoners.

A recent HuffPost/YouGov poll found that few Americans think these efforts have been worthwhile. Only 19 percent of respondents to that poll said that the war on drugs has been worth the costs, while 53 percent said it has not been. That discomfort with the drug war was shared by respondents across the political spectrum.

The question now, experts and advocates say, is just how quickly Washington will catch up to public opinion, and what that shift will mean for the war on drugs and the criminal justice system in general.

The answer could have tremendous ramifications abroad— 10,000 people die drug war deaths every year in Mexico—and at home in the United States.

Demography Is Destiny

Much of the movement in public opinion toward marijuana use has been driven not necessarily by the arguments drug reformers have made for years—that it is safer than alcohol, that we waste too much money on incarceration, that drug use is a victimless crime—but by simple generational change, said Robert Blendon, a professor of health policy and political analysis at Harvard University.

"Younger generations are much more supportive of having choices, they've had much more experience with it, and also in general on many social issues, people are getting more libertarian, more open to less restriction," he said.

In just the past three years, pro-legalization sentiment has spiked 10 percent.

When Blendon studied public opinion on the drug war in the mid-1990s, the results were clear: although the American public believed the drug war was failing, they still thought of using drugs as morally wrong and worthy of punishment.

It was a time when Nancy Reagan's maxim—just say no to drugs—was still treated as gospel. But two decades later, Blendon said, there are simply too many people who have tried marijuana themselves to believe in that.

According to the Pew survey, 48 percent of Americans say they have smoked weed themselves, up 10 percent from a decade ago. Fifty percent of Americans, meanwhile, say smoking marijuana is not a moral issue, compared to 32 percent who believe that it is. That's a mirror image of the 50 percent moral opposition and 35 percent indifference Pew found just seven years ago.

The shift has come fast, Pew found. In just the past three years, pro-legalization sentiment has spiked 10 percent. And a relatively new phenomenon has emerged: it's not just liberals or libertarians speaking out. Increasingly, it is the names most identified with conservatism.

'Right on Crime'

Although President Barack Obama has recently shown signs of "evolving" on marijuana, his Justice Department is still locking up people who grow and distribute weed meant simply for medical use.

In the next few months, Obama will face his moment of truth in the war on drugs: what to do about Colorado and Washington, the two states that legalized marijuana in historic referendums last November. And so far, while legalization and other steps that would help end the drug war are vastly more popular among liberals than conservatives, the president is being outflanked on the right.

In Colorado, former U.S. Rep. Tom Tancredo, known while in office for his strident anti-immigration views, was a prominent supporter of the Amendment 64 referendum legalizing weed on the state level. In the months since the referendum passed, it's become clear that he doesn't stand alone among conservatives.

Robertson, the evangelical media mogul, came out for marijuana legalization at the start of March, citing the staggering human damage of the nation's incarceration system. A couple weeks later, Paul said it wasn't worth putting people in prison for the same crime—smoking marijuana—that both Obama and former President George W. Bush have admitted committing.

While Republicans are still more likely than Democrats to disapprove of marijuana on a moral level—47 to 26 percent, according to Pew—there appears to be a growing sense that it is simply not appropriate, or effective, to lock people up for smoking it.

If a change is to take place, it may have to come on a bipartisan basis, Blendon of Harvard said. "At the moment 30 states have Republican governors, and 24 of them have Republican governors *and* Republican legislatures."

"Obviously we don't support legalizing this," said Marc Levin, director of the Center for Effective Justice at the Texas Public Policy Foundation, which runs an initiative called Right on Crime. "But on some level there's a sense that we have to prioritize—and it's not just a matter of saving money."

Support for marijuana legalization jumped from 30 percent to over 50 percent between 2000 and 2013. But the number of people in federal prison for drug crimes actually grew between 2000 and 2010.

"What we've said is that a couple decades ago, conservatives were right, we were releasing murderers and rapists too early," he said. But "this pendulum swept a bit too broadly, and we swept a lot of nonviolent and low-level offenders into prison."

His group promotes drug courts, treatment options, and "smarter" parole policies as an alternative to the big government, and big tax dollars, approach of prison.

"I think it's a balanced approach that's really appealing to a lot of lawmakers across the spectrum," he said. "There's still the 30-second ad, the bumper sticker, but I do think we're seeing a lot less of the 'soft on crime' rhetoric."

The House Many Still Live In

U.S. drug czar Gil Kerlikowske has shed the term "war on drugs" and has made gestures toward focusing on treatment over incarceration, even while the nation's spending remains tilted toward the latter. But is the war truly ending—and will its most destructive element, the mass incarceration of millions of Americans, end with it?

Although support for marijuana legalization has increased every year over the past decade, the number of people incarcerated in federal prison has only just begun to drop. Support for marijuana legalization jumped from 30 percent to over 50 percent between 2000 and 2013. But the number of people in federal prison for drug crimes actually grew between 2000 and 2010, according to the federal Bureau of Justice Statistics. There were 336,300 people in state and federal jails for drug crimes in 2010.

But there are a number of recent signs that the disconnect between public policy and public opinion is coming to an end. In 2010, Congress passed an act reducing the 18 to 1 sentencing disparity between crack and powder cocaine, which disproportionately affected African-Americans. The ratio is still biased against crack, but less so, an example of the halting and piecemeal progress being made.

This year, meanwhile, Paul and Sen. Patrick Leahy (D-Vt.) introduced a bill that would allow federal judges to override the statutory mandatory minimums that have sent drug offenders away for decades for non-violent offenses.

Yet as Colorado and Washington have shown, change may first come in the states. A host of states are currently considering decriminalizing marijuana, prioritizing treatment instead of imprisonment for drug use, or taking the relatively modest step of making marijuana legal for medical use.

On Monday, filmmaker Eugene Jarecki will screen his documentary about the drug war, *The House I Live In*, for California legislators. The goal is to promote a proposed state bill that would grant prosecutors greater discretion to charge defendants accused of drug possession with lesser crimes.

Change is "snowballing in the right direction," said Tom Angell, chairman of Marijuana Majority. "I think you're going to see a lot of action on the state level in the next several years and action will trickle up to the federal level."

As a student activist, Angell met with members of Congress to argue that students' federal financial aid should not be jeopardized by low-level drug offenses.

"For a long time people would agree with us behind closed doors, but they would be afraid to say that in public," he said. Now, even in Washington, things are changing. "There was just a lot of cynicism and pessimism . . . I think that attitude is really going away."

For decades, the politics of the drug war were straightforward: Being tough could help at the polls and came with no political downside; being open to reform had few advantages, but would be used against a candidate on the campaign trail.

That calculation is no longer so simple. In 2009, Rep. Silvestre Reyes (D-Texas) fought a local El Paso councilman pushing a resolution to discuss legalization as a solution to drug-related border violence. Reyes is now a former congressman. The councilman, Beto O'Rourke, beat him.

The War on Drugs
Is Not Working

Doug Bandow

Doug Bandow is a senior fellow at the Cato Institute, specializing in foreign policy and civil liberties.

Drug use is bad. Arresting people for using drugs is worse. With the states of Colorado and Washington leading the way, the federal government should drop criminal penalties against those who produce, sell, and consume drugs.

The Failure of Drug Prohibition

Prohibition always was a dubious policy for a people who called their country the land of the free. Early restrictions on tobacco and alcohol use failed. The so-called Drug War has been no better. Unfortunately, the latter campaign has always been a violent, often deadly, assault on the American people.

There's no obvious moral reason to demonize the use of mind-altering substances which are widely employed around the globe. Obviously, drugs can be abused, but so can most anything else. That some people will misuse something is no argument for prohibition. Even the Bible only inveighs against alcohol intoxication, not use. In his short book, *The War on Drugs is a War on Freedom*, Christian writer Laurence Vance makes a powerful case against the Drug War.

Some people still may abhor drug use as a matter of personal moral principle, but the criminal law should focus on *interpersonal* morality, that is, behavior which directly affects others. Basing criminal strictures on intra-personal morality essentially puts government into the business of soul-molding, a task for which it has demonstrated little aptitude. And if morality is one's concern, it would be foolish to let politicians make such moral distinctions as celebrating use of alcohol while punishing use of marijuana.

Moreover, whatever one's morals, the Drug War has failed. As Nobel Laureate Milton Friedman observed, "we need not resolve the ethical issue to agree on policy. Prohibition is an attempted cure that makes matters worse for both the addict and the rest of us."

With Uncle Sam effectively bankrupt and many states carrying obligations akin to those of Greece, the Drug War is a wasteful diversion from far more pressing needs.

Drug prohibition has failed in almost every way, leaving extremely high use while yielding all of the counterproductive impacts of criminalization. Our decades-long commitment to legal restrictions has the following real-world impacts. It

- raises drug prices,

- generates enormous profits for criminal entrepreneurs,

- forces even casual consumers into an illegal and often violent market,

- causes heavy users to commit crimes to pay for higher-priced drugs,

- leaves violence as the ultimate arbiter in disputes among users and dealers,

- wastes vast amounts on enforcement efforts,

- corrupts officials and entire institutions, and

- undermines individual liberties.

All this, and drugs remain widely used. If a policy with those outcomes is not a "failure," what would be?

The Impact of the Drug War

The direct enforcement costs run more than $40 billion a year and affect every level of government. Forgone tax revenue is even greater. With Uncle Sam effectively bankrupt and many states carrying obligations akin to those of Greece, the Drug War is a wasteful diversion from far more pressing needs.

Attempting to suppress an enduring and profitable trade also has corrupted virtually every institution it has touched—police, prosecution, judiciary, the Drug Enforcement Agency, and even the military. The problem is even worse in other nations, such as Mexico.

Perhaps the most perverse impact of the Drug War has been to injure and kill users. Far from protecting people from themselves, prohibition actually makes drug use more dangerous. For instance, actor Philip Seymour Hoffman chose to use heroin, but he could never be certain as to its quality, purity, and potency. And he had no way to hold his suppliers accountable for negligently or fraudulently endangering his life. Criminalization also encourages dealers to traffic in substances which are both more concealable and valuable—which usually means more concentrated, and dangerous.

Threatening addicts with jail also makes them less likely to acknowledge their problems and seek assistance. The drug war encourages needle-sharing by IV drug users, which promotes the spread of AIDS and hepatitis. Fear of prosecution causes doctors to under-prescribe painkillers for the sick, while Washington fights to keep marijuana off-limits to the ill, despite evidence that it helps some people suffering from a variety of ailments.

Nor is there any way to run a war against tens of millions of Americans without sacrificing the constitutional liberties of all of us. The drug trade is a classic "self-victim" crime without a complaining witness. Thus, government must rely on intrusive and draconian enforcement procedures: informants, surveillance, wiretaps, and raids. Innocent people are injured and sometimes killed during the increasingly militarized raids.

The Drug War and Crime

Normal constitutional rules don't apply. Lawyers talk of the "drug exception" to the Fourth Amendment. Cops admit to lying to justify arrests. Prosecutors acknowledge relying on dubious testimony to win convictions. Judges apply mandatory minimum penalties for even minimal offenses.

Abundant drug revenues subsidize gangs and organizations which branch out into other crimes, from kidnapping to terrorism.

The crusade against drug use has turned the supposed land of the free into a prison state. Between 1980 and 2000, the number of people under criminal justice control in one form or another *tripled* to six million. Of nearly 14 million arrests in 2009, 1.7 million were for drug crimes, almost *three times* the number arrested for violent offenses. Nearly half of drug arrests were for marijuana. Drug offenders account for more than half of federal convicts. Roughly one fifth of state prisoners are in for drug crimes.

Ironically, the Drug War has created new and more dangerous crimes. The drug laws more than drug use are "crimogenic." For instance, unlike alcohol—which makes one more likely both to commit and be victim of a crime—heroin and marijuana promote passivity. Moreover, by inflating the price of drugs, the Drug War goads addicts to steal.

The worst crimes grow out of a well-funded illegal marketplace. As during Prohibition, violence becomes the ultimate business guarantee. Moreover, abundant drug revenues subsidize gangs and organizations which branch out into other crimes, from kidnapping to terrorism.

The Global Commission on Drug Policy concluded: "increased arrests and law enforcement pressures on drug markets were strongly associated with increased homicide rates and other violent crimes." Even the late [political scientist] James Q. Wilson, who supported drug prohibition, admitted, "It is not clear that enforcing the laws against drug use would reduce crime. On the contrary, crime may be caused by such enforcement." In nations such as Afghanistan, Colombia, Mexico, and Peru, drug trafficking organizations engage in open warfare, often with their respective governments.

The Efficacy of Drug Prohibition

One still could imagine attempting to justify the Drug War if it worked, in the sense of eliminating drug use. However, drug prohibition has accomplished little in this regard, having the most impact where it is least needed. Observed [economist] Mary M. Cleveland: "Most people choose not to use illicit drugs even when they have cheap and easy access to them. Enforcement can have some effect on light users; regular and problem users will get their drugs even in prison. Drug treatment and changes in social norms have far more influence on drug use than enforcement because they affect individuals' attitudes."

Government figures indicate that nearly half of Americans older than 12 have tried illegal drugs. Tens of millions of people use with some regularity. High school students report that drugs are easily accessible. Drug use persists even in countries where governments execute dealers.

Ironically, there is no correlation between increased enforcement and decreased consumption. The *Economist* magazine observed: "There is no correlation between the harshness of drug laws and the incidence of drug-taking: citizens living under tough regimes (notably America but also Britain) take more drugs, not fewer."

The Benefits of Drug Legalization

Frustration with the Drug War obviously was manifested in the decision by voters in Colorado and Washington to legalize recreational marijuana use. Uruguay has done the same, with pressure rising in other Latin American nations to shift away from prohibition. Former presidents of Brazil, Colombia, and Mexico are urging a "Drug Peace."

Cocaine, heroin, and marijuana once were legal in the U.S., but America did not turn into a nation of addicts.

America's states could experiment. Drugs could be sold with varying restrictions (such as we impose on alcohol and tobacco). The specific treatment of individual substances could be based on assessments of harm and the possible impact on others.

Greatest law enforcement efforts should remain directed at kids. That actually would be easier in a semi-legal gray rather than illegal black market.

Legalization would not be a scary jump into the unknown. Portugal decriminalized all drugs a decade ago. Great Britain, the Netherlands, and Switzerland have permitted some legal drug use. Cocaine, heroin, and marijuana once were legal in the U.S., but America did not turn into a nation of addicts. A dozen American states previously decriminalized marijuana use and many more have legalized the use of medical marijuana. While these policies have not been problem-free, none have seen challenges approaching those caused by criminal prohibition.

Indeed, the upside potential of legalization is enormous. [Social psychologist] Robert MacCoun and [criminologist] Peter Reuter wrote in *Drug War Heresies*, "Reductions in criminal sanctioning have little or no effect on the prevalence of drug use (i.e., the number of users)." Even if "relaxed drug laws increase the prevalence of use . . ., the additional users will, on average, use less heavily and less harmfully than those who would have also used drugs under prohibition."

People should not abuse drugs. It might be best if they didn't use them at all. However, that is no justification for a war against drug users, arresting many and endangering all. Indeed, we all pay the price from increased crime and decreased liberties.

American governments at all levels should terminate the Drug War. It is time to stop treating the American people as the enemy.

Prohibition of Marijuana Unnecessarily Criminalizes Young Minorities

Harry Levine

Harry Levine is professor of sociology at Queens College and the Graduate Center, City University of New York.

"Whites Smoke Pot, but Blacks Are Arrested." That was the headline of a column by Jim Dwyer, the great Metro desk reporter for *The New York Times*, in December 2009. Although Dwyer was writing about New York City, he summed up perfectly two central and enduring facts about marijuana use and arrests across the country: whites and blacks use marijuana equally, but the police do not arrest them equally. A third important fact: the vast majority (76 percent) of those arrested and charged with the crime of marijuana possession are young people in their teens and 20s.

Arrests for Marijuana Possession

Over the last fifteen years, police departments in the United States made 10 million arrests for marijuana possession—an average of almost 700,000 arrests a year. Police arrest blacks for marijuana possession at higher rates than whites in every state and nearly every city and county—as FBI Uniform Crime Reports and state databases indisputably show. States with the largest racial disparities arrest blacks at six times the rate of whites. This list includes Alabama, Illinois, Iowa, Kansas, Kentucky, Minnesota, Pennsylvania, Nebraska, Nevada, New York and Wisconsin.

Harry Levine, "The Scandal of Racist Marijuana Arrests—and What To Do About It." Reprinted with permission from the November 18, 2013 issue of *The Nation*. For subscription information, call 1-800-333-8536. Portions of each week's Nation magazine can be accessed at http://www.thenation.com.

Big city police departments are among the worst offenders. Police in Los Angeles, Chicago and New York have arrested blacks for marijuana possession at more than seven times the rate of whites. Since 1997, New York City alone has arrested and jailed more than 600,000 people for possessing marijuana; about 87 percent of the arrests are of blacks and Latinos. For years, police in New York and Chicago have arrested more young blacks and Latinos for simple marijuana possession than for any other criminal offense whatsoever.

Other large urban areas that make huge numbers of racially biased arrests include Atlanta, Baltimore, Buffalo, Cleveland, Dallas-Fort Worth, Detroit, Fort Lauderdale, Houston, Las Vegas, Memphis, Miami, Nashville, Philadelphia, St. Louis, Tampa and Washington, DC. And across the United States, one-third of marijuana arrestees are teenagers; 62 percent are age 24 or younger; and most of them are ordinary high school or college students and young workers.

This is not a problem of training or supervision or rogue squads or bad apples. It's a systemic problem, a form of institutional racism created and administered by people at the highest levels of law enforcement and government.

The essential study of these possession arrests and their pervasive racial bias is *The War on Marijuana in Black and White*, an extraordinary book-length report released by the ACLU [American Civil Liberties Union] earlier this year. It found that police arrest blacks for marijuana possession at higher rates than whites in poor, middle-class and wealthy communities (with richer counties showing the greatest bias). The glaring racial disparities in marijuana arrests are "as staggering in the Midwest as in the Northeast, in large counties as in small, on city streets as on country roads. . . . They exist regardless of whether blacks make up 50% or 5% of a county's overall population."

Young whites (age 18 to 25), however, use marijuana more than young blacks, and government studies comparing marijuana use among whites and blacks of all ages have found that both groups use it at a similar rate.

A Systematic Problem

Why are marijuana arrests so racially skewed? Such dramatic and widespread racial disparities are clearly not the product of personal prejudice or racism on the part of individual police officers. This is not a problem of training or supervision or rogue squads or bad apples. It's a systemic problem, a form of institutional racism created and administered by people at the highest levels of law enforcement and government.

Most people arrested for marijuana possession were *not* smoking it: they typically had a small amount hidden in their clothing, vehicle or personal effects. The police found the marijuana by stopping and searching them (often illegally), or by tricking them into revealing it.

Police departments concentrate their patrols only in certain neighborhoods, usually ones designated as "high crime." These are mainly places where low-income whites and people of color live. In these neighborhoods, police stop and search the most vehicles and individuals while looking for "contraband" of any type to make an arrest. The most common item that people in any neighborhood possess that will get them arrested—and the most common item that police find—is a small amount of marijuana.

Police officers patrolling in middle- and upper-middle-class neighborhoods typically do not search the vehicles and pockets of white people, so most well-off whites enjoy a de facto legalization of marijuana possession. Free from the intense surveillance and frequent searches that occur in other neighborhoods, they have little reason to fear a humiliating arrest and incarceration. This produces patterns, as in Chicago, where whites constitute 45 percent of the population but only 5 percent of those arrested for possession.

The result has been called "racism without racists." No individual officers need harbor racial animosity for the criminal justice system to produce jails and courts filled with black and brown faces. But the absence of hostile intent does not absolve policy-makers and law enforcement officials from responsibility or blame. As federal judge Shira Scheindlin recently determined in two prominent stop-and-frisk cases, New York City's top officials "adopted an attitude of willful blindness toward statistical evidence of racial disparities in stops and stop outcomes." She cited the legal doctrine of "deliberate indifference" to describe police and city officials who "willfully ignored overwhelming proof that the policy . . . is racially discriminatory and therefore violates the United States Constitution."

To an extraordinary extent, middle-class and especially upper-middle-class and wealthy white Americans have been shielded from information about . . . the policing of marijuana possession.

A Problematic Invisibility

Racially biased marijuana enforcement stretches far beyond New York City—and its pernicious effects extend far beyond the degrading experience of being arrested and jailed. Most serious are the lifelong criminal records produced by a single arrest. Twenty years ago, misdemeanor arrest records were papers stored in dusty file cabinets. Now they are computerized and instantly available for $20 or less from commercial database firms—and easily found by a Google search for the phrase "criminal records." (Try it yourself.) Employers, landlords, schools, banks and credit card companies rule out applicants on the basis of these now universally available records, which have been aptly described as a "scarlet letter" and a "new Jim Crow." The substantial damage caused by criminal records from the millions of marijuana arrests has also been willfully disregarded by top officials almost everywhere, including in Congress and the White House.

Perhaps surprisingly, police departments, prosecutors and elected officials rarely discuss their marijuana arrests. They don't take credit for—or try to justify—arresting and jailing people in record-breaking numbers for possession. In fact, they usually seek to keep marijuana arrests out of the public eye.

This makes it difficult for many white Americans to believe that so many people are being arrested for possessing small amounts of marijuana. The news media don't report on these cases; nor are white Americans likely to personally know anyone who has been arrested (or whose children have been arrested) for marijuana possession. To an extraordinary extent, middle-class and especially upper-middle-class and wealthy white Americans have been shielded from information about—and remain unaffected by—the policing of marijuana possession. The near-invisibility of these arrests has also hidden the strong support for them by police departments and prosecutors.

The Crusade Against Marijuana

The national crusade against marijuana can be traced to the early 1990s, as the "war on drugs" shifted its focus from crack cocaine to marijuana under Bill Clinton. Since then, Congress has regularly allocated billions in federal funding to local police and prosecutors under the Justice Department's anti-drug and police programs. Grantees often report their drug possession arrests as evidence of their accomplishments using these funds—and as proof that they should receive more. Federal money has thus subsidized the arrests of millions of young people for possessing marijuana, disproportionately young people of color. Prominent blue-state Democrats like Joe Biden, Dianne Feinstein, Charles Schumer, Hillary Clinton and Barack Obama have strongly supported these grants over the years; in 2009, the fiscal stimulus actually doubled the anti-drug funding for local law enforcement agencies.

For ordinary patrol officers, marijuana arrests are relatively safe and easy work.

More than many people realize, prominent liberals have long been among law enforcement's most important political allies. A substantial power bloc of "drug war liberals"—or what might more broadly be termed "law-and-order liberals"—has played a major role in sustaining this drug war policing. Police departments depend on liberal Democrats to defend their funding and policy needs. Liberals in Congress and the White House, in turn, depend on police lobbying groups to support important legislation, such as their endorsement of immigration and gun reforms. And politicians at all levels of government gain credibility with many voters by having top police officials vouch for their steadfastness in "fighting crime."

With this federal support and encouragement, arrests for marijuana possession climbed from a crack-era low of 260,000 in 1990, to 500,000 in 1995, to 640,000 in 2000, to 690,000 in 2005, to 750,000 in 2010. The ACLU calculates that these arrests have cost taxpayers at least $3.6 billion a year. And there is absolutely no evidence that they reduce serious or violent crime—or even drug use.

The Benefit to Law Enforcement

So the question again becomes: Why? Why have these millions of arrests happened? Why is it so hard to stop them? While federal funding and drug war propaganda have helped drive marijuana arrests, police and sheriffs' departments have had their own reasons to embrace and fiercely defend the practice.

Central to understanding the national marijuana arrest crusade is the fact that significant constituencies within police departments benefit from marijuana arrests, find them useful for internal departmental purposes, and want them to continue.

For ordinary patrol officers, marijuana arrests are relatively safe and easy work. Policing can be dangerous, but officers are unlikely to get shot or stabbed while searching and arresting teenagers for marijuana possession. All police departments have formal and informal activity quotas; in many departments, officers can show productivity and earn overtime pay by stopping and searching ten or so young people near the end of a shift and making a marijuana arrest. Police officers in New York have long used the term "collars for dollars" to refer to the practice of making misdemeanor arrests to earn overtime pay. Also, from the officers' point of view, people possessing marijuana are highly desirable arrestees. As one veteran lieutenant put it, they are "clean"; unlike drunks and heroin addicts, young marijuana users rarely have HIV, hepatitis, tuberculosis or even body lice. They are unlikely to throw up on the officer, in the patrol car or at the station. Marijuana arrests are indeed a quality-of-life issue—for the police.

Most important, police department supervisors at all levels find that marijuana possession arrests are very useful. They are proof of productivity to their superiors; some supervisors also receive overtime pay for the extra work by officers under their command. Making many searches and arrests for minor offenses is also excellent training for rookie police. If a new officer screws up the paperwork, it doesn't matter because, as one sergeant explained, "it's just a pot arrest." And if a crisis or emergency comes up, police commanders can temporarily reassign officers making arrests for marijuana without hindering an ongoing investigation. This "reserve army" of police focusing on petty offenses keeps officers busy, provides records of their whereabouts and productivity, and gives commanders staffing flexibility.

Marijuana arrests also enable police department managers to obtain fingerprints, photographs and other data on young people who would not otherwise end up in their databases. There is nothing else the police can do that gets so many new people into their system as the broad net of marijuana possession arrests.

When possession becomes a "noncriminal" offense but still an illegal one, local law enforcement agencies often continue many of the same practices as before.

Police officials and managers have become so dependent on marijuana arrests that one could reasonably conclude that their departments are addicted to them. And they don't want to give up their habit. In recent years, police agencies, prosecutors' offices, and their influential network of political and lobbying organizations have emerged as the chief opponents of drug-law reform. It is not the religious right, or anti-drug groups, or even the drug treatment industry that lobbies and campaigns against marijuana ballot initiatives and legislative drug-law reforms. Rather, law enforcement organizations are leading the charge as well as providing the troops to defend the drug war.

The Solution of Equal Policing for All

The ACLU's report emphatically calls for an end to marijuana possession arrests, noting that the only way to accomplish this is by legalizing the possession and use of marijuana, and ultimately by regulating its production and sale.

Although the decriminalization of marijuana possession has been implemented in countries with a national police system, in the United States this has turned out to be a false solution. When possession becomes a "noncriminal" offense but still an illegal one, local law enforcement agencies often continue many of the same practices as before—but now without public defenders to represent the young people charged with a "drug offense," and without public data to document what police, prosecutors and courts are doing. Some police departments simply ignore the decriminalization laws, as the NYPD [New York Police Department] has done for over fifteen years.

However, as Colorado and Washington have proved in just the last year, there is a very good alternative: even without instituting commercial sale, the legalization of marijuana can stop most of these possession arrests.

The larger goal of ending punitive and biased drug arrests requires seismic changes in law enforcement: it will mean creating policing for a post-drug war America. One reform that makes others possible is guaranteeing public access to much more aggregate criminal justice data, both historical and current. With it, researchers and journalists can reveal routine police, prosecutor and court practices, as some of us have been doing for marijuana arrests and stop-and-frisks.

One way of conceptualizing these changes is to view them as bringing the civil rights movement to policing policies. In the last two decades, police department staff have become increasingly racially integrated. But in many cities and counties, the day-to-day practices of police and sheriffs' departments are still determined by the race, class and ethnicity of a neighborhood's residents. Despite the many successes of the civil rights movement, we continue to live within two worlds of policing, separate and unequal: one for middle-class and wealthier people, the other for poorer Americans and, especially, people of color.

It is time for America to fully embrace equal policing for all. Unfortunately, like all humane, just and progressive change, this will not be granted. It must be won.

The Prohibition of Drugs Is Working and Should Continue

John P. Walters

John P. Walters is the former director of the White House Office of National Drug Control Policy.

You might have missed it, but on July 9 [2013] the White House quietly announced in a press release that cocaine use in the U.S. is down by over a third since 2006. This news comes on the heels of a major reduction in world-wide cocaine production, down 41% between 2001 and 2012 according to the Office of National Drug Control Policy. Cocaine-related deaths in the U.S. dropped 44% between 2006 and 2010. The rate of positive drug tests for cocaine declined even more steeply, down 65% between 2006 and mid-2012.

Success in Controlling Illegal Drugs

You do not have to have lived during the cocaine and crack epidemics of the 1980s and early 1990s to be grateful for this remarkable change. If you did, the progress seems miraculous. Unfortunately, the Obama administration is cutting the funds and undermining the political will that helped bring about this transformation.

Of all those who contributed to this striking success in the effort to control illegal drugs, two leaders deserve particular thanks: Alvaro Uribe, president of Colombia from 2002–10, and Felipe Calderón, president of Mexico from 2006–12.

President Uribe changed the future of Colombia by attacking the cocaine trade and violent groups on the left and right who used trafficking as a source of power. He brought the rule of law to large areas of his country where people had given up hope.

President Calderón made taking back Mexico from violent traffickers—narco-terrorists—the center of his administration. While cocaine trafficking is only a part of the cartels' criminal activity, Mr. Calderón stepped up attacks on cartel leaders; in January 2007 he even sent a planeload of his worst traffickers to justice in the United States. Because he had the courage to take on this difficult struggle, he began to see the power and violence of these criminal groups decline before he left office, as drug-related murders dropped 12% in the first five months of 2012.

An Alliance with the United States

Messrs. Uribe and Calderón created an unprecedented alliance with the U.S. to serve the interests of their homelands, but as in any true alliance all the partners were better for it. Democrats and Republicans stood up for these two leaders, giving critical enforcement, eradication, interdiction and adjudication support to their efforts. During their presidencies, Colombia and Mexico extradited hundreds of their worst traffickers to the U.S. to buy time for their developing judicial systems.

President Obama's failure to push back against drug legalization in this country works against international anti-drug efforts.

Recent events in Mexico indicate that enforcement successes there will be sustained. But Mr. Calderón has expressed frustration with the failure to reduce drug consumption in the U.S., and he has warned that unchecked demand could lead to drug legalization.

A 41% reduction in cocaine production, one might imagine, has something to do with a 44% reduction in cocaine overdoses. Yet the Obama administration is actually proposing to cut funding for international drug control to $1.5 billion for fiscal year 2014 from $1.9 billion in this fiscal year, a 21% reduction. In its July 9 press release, the White House tells us that it is time to spend an additional $1.4 billion to expand treatment and education, "the largest percentage increase in at least two decades."

The Need to Fight Against Drug Legalization

Prevention and treatment are worthy activities, but the administration seems to have missed the point in its press release, which links the declines in cocaine use to reductions in supply. It offers no evidence that treatment and prevention played any role.

Most of all, President Obama's failure to push back against drug legalization in this country works against international anti-drug efforts. Raymond Yans, president of the International Narcotics Control Board, warned in March that allowing the implementation of legalization initiatives in Colorado and Washington "would be a violation of international law, namely the United Nations Single Convention on Narcotic Drugs, to which the United States is a party." The U.S. is now undermining the foundation of the very achievement the administration just announced.

President Obama is as close to an icon for the young as any president has ever been. He and many of his generation used drugs and suffered for that use—a point he makes in his 1995 autobiography, *Dreams From My Father.*

The president needs once again to speak honestly about the danger. If he sat with our children and spoke to them as if they were his daughters, he would be a powerful force for prevention. How about a single speech? Perhaps he could dedicate it to America's allies and the brave men and women who have given their lives to keep us safe.

Drug Legalisation: An Evaluation of the Impacts on Global Society

Drug Free America Foundation, Inc.

The Drug Free America Foundation, Inc. is a drug prevention and policy organization committed to reducing illegal drug use and drug addiction.

Various well funded pressure groups have mounted campaigns to overturn the United Nations Conventions on drugs. These groups claim that society should accept the fact of drugs as a problem that will remain and, therefore, should be managed in a way that would enable millions of people to take advantage of an alleged 'legal right' to use drugs of their choice.

It is important to note that international law makes a distinction between "hard law" and "soft law." Hard law is legally binding upon the States. Soft law is not binding. UN Conventions, such as the Conventions on Drugs, are considered hard law and must be upheld by the countries that have ratified the UN Drug Conventions.

International narcotics legislation is mainly made up of the three UN Conventions from 1961 (Single Convention on Narcotic Drugs), 1971 (Convention on Psychotropic Substances), and 1988 (Convention against Illicit Traffic in Narcotic Drugs and Psychotropic Substances):

- The 1961 Convention sets out that "the possession, use, trade in, distribution, import, export, manufacture and the production of drugs is exclusively limited to medical and scientific purposes". Penal cooperation is to be established so as to ensure that drugs are only used licitly (for prescribed medical purposes).

- The 1971 Convention resembles closely the 1961 Convention, whilst establishing an international control system for Psychotropic Substances.

- The 1988 Convention reflects the response of the international community to increasing illicit cultivation, production, manufacture, and trafficking activities.

International narcotics legislation draws a line between licit (medical) and illicit (non-medical) use, and sets out measures for prevention of illicit use, including penal measures. The preamble to the 1961 Convention states that the parties to the Convention are "Recognizing that addiction to narcotic drugs constitutes a serious evil for the individual and is fraught with social and economic danger to mankind". The Conventions are reviewed every ten years and have consistently been upheld.

The UN system of drug control includes the Office of Drugs and Crime, the International Narcotics Control Board, and the Commission on Narcotic Drugs. The works of these bodies are positive and essential in international drug demand and supply reduction. They are also attacked by those seeking to legalise drugs.

Through this ill-informed propaganda, people are asked to believe that [drug legalisation] would defeat the traffickers, take the profit out of the drug trade and solve the drug problem completely.

It is frequently and falsely asserted that the so-called "War on Drugs" is inappropriate and has become a very costly and demonstrable failure. It is declared by some that vast resources have been poured into the prevention of drug use and the suppression of illicit manufacturing, trafficking, and supply. It is further claimed that what is essentially a chronic medical problem has been turned into a criminal justice issue with inappropriate remedies that make "innocent" people criminals. In short, the flawed argument is that "prohibition" monies have been wasted and the immeasurable financial resources applied to this activity would be better spent for the general benefit of the community.

The groups supporting legalisation are: people who use drugs, those who believe that the present system of control does more harm than good, and those who are keen to make significant profits from marketing newly authorised addictive substances. In addition to pernicious distribution of drugs, dealers circulate specious and misleading information. They foster the erroneous belief that drugs are harmless, thus adding to even more confused thinking.

Superficially crafted, yet pseudo-persuasive arguments are put forward that can be accepted by many concerned, well intentioned people who have neither the time nor the knowledge to research the matter thoroughly, but accept them in good faith. Frequently high profile people claim that legalisation is the best way of addressing a major social problem without cogent supporting evidence. This too influences others, especially the ill-informed who accept statements as being accurate and well informed. Through this ill-informed propaganda, people are asked to believe that such action would defeat the traffickers, take the profit out of the drug trade and solve the drug problem completely.

The total case for legalisation seems to be based on the assertion that the government assault on alleged civil liberties has been disastrously and expensively ineffective and counterproductive. In short, it is alleged, in contradiction to evidence, that prohibition has produced more costs than benefits and, therefore, the use of drugs on a personal basis should be permitted. Advocates claim that legalisation would eliminate the massive expenditure incurred by prohibition and would take the profit out of crime for suppliers and dealers. They further claim that it would decriminalise what they consider "understandable" human behaviour and thus prevent the overburdening of the criminal justice system that is manifestly failing to cope. It is further argued irrationally that police time would not be wasted on minor drug offences, the courts would be freed from the backlog of trivial cases and the prisons would not be used as warehouses for those who choose to use drugs, and the saved resources could be used more effectively.

Legalisation of current illicit drugs, including marijuana, is not a viable solution to the global drug problem and would actually exacerbate the problem.

Types of Drug Legalisation

The term "legalisation" can have any one of the following meanings:

1. *Total Legalisation*—All illicit drugs such as heroin, cocaine, methamphetamine, and marijuana would be legal and treated as commercial products. No government regulation would be required to oversee production, marketing, or distribution.

2. *Regulated Legalisation*—The production and distribution of drugs would be regulated by the government with limits on amounts that can be purchased and the age of purchasers. There would be no criminal or civil sanctions for possessing, manufacturing, or distributing drugs unless these actions violated the regulatory system. Drug sales could be taxed.

3. *Decriminalisation*—Decriminalisation eliminates criminal sanctions for drug use and provides civil sanctions for possession of drugs.

To achieve the agenda of drug legalisation, advocates argue for:

- legalising drugs by lowering or ending penalties for drug possession and use—particularly marijuana;

- legalising marijuana and other illicit drugs as a so-called medicine;

- harm reduction programmes such as needle exchange programmes, drug injection sites, heroin distribution to addicts, and facilitation of so-called safe use of drugs that normalize drug use, create the illusion that drugs can be used safely if one just knows how, and eliminates a goal of abstinence from drugs;

- legalised growing of industrial hemp;

- an inclusion of drug users as equal partners in establishing and enforcing drug policy; and

- protection for drug users at the expense and to the detriment of non-users under the pretense of "human rights."

The Problem Is with the Drugs and Not the Drug Policies

Legalisation of current illicit drugs, including marijuana, is not a viable solution to the global drug problem and would actually exacerbate the problem.

The UN Drug Conventions were adopted because of the recognition by the international community that drugs are an enormous social problem and that the trade adversely affects the global economy and the viability of some countries that have become transit routes. The huge sums of illegal money generated by the drug trade encourage money laundering and have become inextricably linked with other international organised criminal activities such as terrorism, human trafficking, prostitution and the arms trade. Drug Lords have subverted the democratic governments of some countries to the great detriment of law abiding citizens.

We . . . urge our leaders to reject the legalisation of currently illicit drugs as an acceptable solution to the world's drug problem.

Drug abuse has had a major adverse effect on global health and the spread of communicable diseases such as AIDS/HIV. Control is vitally important for the protection of communities against these problems.

There is international agreement in the UN Conventions that drugs should be produced legally under strict supervision to ensure adequate supplies only for *medical* and *research* purposes. The cumulative effects of prohibition and interdiction combined with education and treatment during 100 years of international drug control have had a significant impact in stemming the drug problem. Control is working and one can only imagine how much worse the problem would have become without it. For instance:

- In 2007, drug control had reduced the global opium supply to one-third the level in 1907 and even though current reports indicate recent increased cultivation in Afghanistan and production in Southeast Asia, overall production has not increased.

- During the last decade, world output of cocaine and amphetamines has stabilized; cannabis output has declined since 2004; and opium production has declined since 2008.

We, therefore, strongly urge nations to uphold and enhance current efforts to prevent the use, cultivation, production, traffic, and sale of illegal drugs. We further urge our leaders to reject the legalisation of currently illicit drugs as an acceptable solution to the world's drug problem because of the following reasons:

- Only 6.1% of people globally between the ages of 15 and 64 use drugs (World Drug Report 2011 UNODC) and there is little public support for the legalisation of highly dangerous substances. Prohibition has ensured that the total number of users is low because legal sanctions do influence people's behaviour.

- There is a specific obligation to protect children from the harms of drugs, as is evidenced through the ratification by the majority of United Nations Member States of the UN Convention on the Rights of the Child (CRC). Article 33 states that Member States "shall take all appropriate measures, including legislative, administrative, social and educational measures, to protect children from the illicit use of narcotic drugs and psychotropic substances as defined in the relevant international treaties, and to prevent the use of children in the illicit production and trafficking of such substances".

- Legalisation sends the dangerous tacit message of approval, that drug use is acceptable and cannot be very harmful.

- Permissibility, availability and accessibility of dangerous drugs will result in increased consumption by many who otherwise would not consider using them.

- Enforcement of laws creates risks that discourage drug use. Laws clearly define what is legal and illegal and emphasise the boundaries.

- Legalisation would increase the risks to individuals, families, communities and world regions without any compensating benefits.

- Legalisation would remove the social sanctions normally supported by a legal system and expose people to additional risk, especially the young and vulnerable.

- The legalisation of drugs would lead inevitably to a greater number of dependencies and addictions likely to match the levels of licit addictive substances. In turn, this would lead to increasing related morbidity and mortality, the spread of communicable diseases such as AIDS/HIV and the other blood borne viruses exacerbated by the sharing of needles and drugs paraphernalia, and an increased burden on the health and social services.

- There would be no diminution in criminal justice costs as, contrary to the view held by those who support legalisation, crime would not be eliminated or reduced. Dependency often brings with it dysfunctional families together with increased domestic child abuse.

- There will be increases in drugged driving and industrial accidents.

- Drug Control is a safeguard protecting millions from the effects of drug abuse and addiction particularly, but not exclusively, in developing countries.

- Statements about taxation offsetting any additional costs are demonstrably flawed and this has been shown in the case of alcohol and tobacco taxes. Short of governments distributing free drugs, those who commit crime now to obtain them would continue to do so if they became legal.

- Legalisation would not take the profit out of the drug trade as criminals will always find ways of countering legislation. They would continue their dangerous activities including cutting drugs with harmful substances to maximise sales and profits. Aggressive marketing techniques, designed to promote increased sales and use, would be applied rigorously to devastating effect.

- Other 'legal' drugs—alcohol and tobacco, are regularly traded on the black market and are an international smuggling problem; an estimated 600 billion cigarettes are smuggled annually (World Drug report 2009). Taxation monies raised from these products go nowhere near addressing consequential costs.

- Many prisons have become incubators for infection and the spread of drug related diseases at great risk to individual prisoners, prison staff and the general public. Failure to eliminate drug use in these institutions exacerbates the problem.

- The prisons are not full of people who have been convicted for mere possession of drugs for personal use. This sanction is usually reserved for dealers and those who commit crime in the furtherance of their possession.

- The claim that alcohol and tobacco may cause more harm than some drugs is not a justification for legalising other dangerous substances. The pharmacology and pharmacokinetics of psychotropic substances suggest that more, not less, control of their access is warranted.

- Research regularly and increasingly demonstrates the harms associated with drug use and misuse. There is uncertainty, yet growing evidence, about the long-term detrimental effects of drug use on the physical, psychological and emotional health of substance users.

- It is inaccurate to suggest that the personal use of drugs has no consequential and damaging effects. Apart from the harm to the individual users, drugs affect others by addiction, violence, criminal behaviour and road accidents. Some drugs remain in the body for long periods and adversely affect performance and behaviour beyond the time of so-called 'private' use. Legalisation would not diminish the adverse effects associated with drug misuse such as criminal, irrational and violent behaviour and the mental and physical harm that occurs in many users.

- All drugs can be dangerous including prescription and over the counter medicines if they are taken without attention to medical guidance. Recent research has confirmed just how harmful drug use can be and there is now overwhelming evidence (certainly in the case of cannabis) to make consideration of legalisation irresponsible.

- The toxicity of drugs is not a matter for debate or a vote. People are entitled to their own opinions but not their own facts. Those who advocate freedom of choice cannot create freedom from adverse consequences.

- Drug production causes huge ecological damage and crop erosion in drug producing areas.

- Nearly every nation has signed the UN Conventions on drug control. Any government of signatory countries contemplating legalisation would be in breach of agreements under the UN Conventions which recognise that unity is the best approach to combating the global drug problem. The administrative burden associated with legalisation would become enormous and probably unaffordable to most governments. Legalisation would require a massive government commitment to production, supply, security and a bureaucracy that would necessarily increase the need for the employment at great and unaffordable cost for all of the staff necessary to facilitate that development.

- Any government policy must be motivated by the consideration that it must first do no harm. There is an obligation to protect citizens and the compassionate and sensible method must be to do everything possible to reduce drug dependency and misuse, not to encourage or facilitate it. Any failures in a common approach to a problem would result in a complete breakdown in effectiveness. Differing and fragmented responses to a common predicament are unacceptable for the wellbeing of the international community. It is incumbent on national governments to cooperate in securing the greatest good for the greatest number.

CHAPTER 2

Is Drug Use Dangerous for Society?

Overview: Drug Use in the United States

Substance Abuse and Mental Health Services Administration

The Substance Abuse and Mental Health Services Administration (SAMHSA) is the agency within the US Department of Health and Human Services that leads public health efforts to advance the behavioral health of all Americans.

In 2012, an estimated 23.9 million Americans aged 12 or older were current (past month) illicit drug users, meaning they had used an illicit drug during the month prior to the survey interview. This estimate represents 9.2 percent of the population aged 12 or older. Illicit drugs include marijuana/hashish, cocaine (including crack), heroin, hallucinogens, inhalants, or prescription-type psychotherapeutics (pain relievers, tranquilizers, stimulants, and sedatives) used nonmedically.

The Rate of Illicit Drug Use

The rate of current illicit drug use among persons aged 12 or older increased from 8.1 percent in 2008 to 9.2 percent in 2012. The rate in 2012 was similar to the rates in 2009 to 2011 (ranging from 8.7 to 8.9 percent), but it was higher than the rates in the years from 2002 to 2008 (ranging from 7.9 to 8.3 percent).

Marijuana was the most commonly used illicit drug. In 2012, there were 18.9 million past month users. Between 2007 and 2012, the rate of current use increased from 5.8 to 7.3 percent, and the number of users increased from 14.5 million to 18.9 million.

Substance Abuse and Mental Health Services Administration, "Results from the 2012 National Survey on Drug Use and Health: Summary of National Findings," 2013, pp. 1–2.

Daily or almost daily use of marijuana (used on 20 or more days in the past month) increased from 5.1 million persons in 2007 to 7.6 million persons in 2012.

In 2012, there were 1.6 million current cocaine users aged 12 or older, comprising 0.6 percent of the population. These estimates were similar to the number and rate in 2011 (1.4 million persons and 0.5 percent), but they were lower than in 2003 to 2007 (e.g., 2.4 million persons and 1.0 percent in 2006).

The number of past year heroin users increased between 2007 (373,000) and 2012 (669,000).

Among youths aged 12 to 17, the current illicit drug use rate was similar in 2011 (10.1 percent) and 2012 (9.5 percent).

An estimated 1.1 million persons aged 12 or older in 2012 (0.4 percent) used hallucinogens in the past month. These estimates were similar to the estimates in 2002 to 2011.

The percentage of persons aged 12 or older who used prescription-type psychotherapeutic drugs nonmedically in the past month in 2012 (2.6 percent) was similar to the percentage in 2011 (2.4 percent) and all years from 2002 through 2010.

The number of past month methamphetamine users decreased between 2006 and 2012, from 731,000 (0.3 percent) to 440,000 (0.2 percent).

Drug Use Among Youths and Young Adults

Among youths aged 12 to 17, the current illicit drug use rate was similar in 2011 (10.1 percent) and 2012 (9.5 percent). The rate declined from 11.6 percent in 2002 to 9.3 percent in 2008, increased to 10.1 percent in 2009, and remained at 10.1 percent in 2010 and 2011.

The rate of current marijuana use among youths aged 12 to 17 decreased from 8.2 percent in 2002 to 6.7 percent in 2006, remained unchanged at 6.7 percent in 2007 and 2008, then increased to 7.9 percent in 2011. The rate declined to 7.2 percent in 2012.

Among youths aged 12 to 17, the rate of current non-medical use of prescription-type drugs declined from 4.0 percent in 2002 to 2.8 percent in 2012. The rate of nonmedical pain reliever use declined during this period from 3.2 to 2.2 percent among youths.

The rate of current use of illicit drugs among young adults aged 18 to 25 increased from 19.7 percent in 2008 to 21.3 percent in 2012, driven largely by an increase in marijuana use (from 16.6 percent in 2008 to 18.7 percent in 2012).

Among young adults aged 18 to 25, the rate of current nonmedical use of prescription-type drugs in 2012 was 5.3 percent, which was similar to the rates in 2010 and 2011, but it was lower than the rate in the years from 2003 to 2007 (ranging from 5.9 to 6.5 percent).

There was a decrease from 2005 to 2012 in the use of cocaine among young adults aged 18 to 25, from 2.6 to 1.1 percent.

Adult Drug Use

Among adults aged 50 to 64, the rate of current illicit drug use increased during the past decade. For adults aged 50 to 54, the rate increased from 3.4 percent in 2002 to 7.2 percent in 2012. Among those aged 55 to 59, the rate of current illicit drug use increased from 1.9 percent in 2002 to 6.6 percent in 2012. Among those aged 60 to 64, the rate increased from 1.1 percent in 2003 to 3.6 percent in 2012. These trends partially reflect the aging into these age groups of members of the baby boom cohort (i.e., persons born between 1946 and 1964), whose rates of illicit drug use have been higher than those of older cohorts.

Among unemployed adults aged 18 or older in 2012, 18.1 percent were current illicit drug users, which was higher than the rates of 8.9 percent for those who were employed full time and 12.5 percent for those who were employed part time. However, most illicit drug users were employed. Of the 21.5 million current illicit drug users aged 18 or older in 2012, 14.6 million (67.9 percent) were employed either full or part time.

In 2012, 10.3 million persons aged 12 or older reported driving under the influence of illicit drugs during the past year. This corresponds to 3.9 percent of the population aged 12 or older, which was higher than the rate in 2011 (3.7 percent). The rate had declined steadily between 2002 and 2011, from 4.7 to 3.7 percent, before increasing in 2012. In 2012, the rate was highest among young adults aged 18 to 25 (11.9 percent).

Among persons aged 12 or older in 2011–2012 who used pain relievers nonmedically in the past 12 months, 54.0 percent got the drug they used most recently from a friend or relative for free, and 10.9 percent bought the drug from a friend or relative. Another 19.7 percent reported that they got the drug through a prescription from one doctor. An annual average of 4.3 percent got pain relievers from a drug dealer or other stranger, and 0.2 percent bought them on the Internet.

Marijuana Use Harms Health and Is Addictive

National Institute on Drug Abuse

The National Institute on Drug Abuse is part of the National Institutes of Health of the US Department of Health and Human Services, providing national leadership for research on drug abuse and addiction.

Marijuana refers to the dried leaves, flowers, stems, and seeds from the hemp plant *Cannabis sativa*, which contains the psychoactive (mind-altering) chemical delta-9-tetrahydrocannabinol (THC), as well as other related compounds. This plant material can also be concentrated in a resin called *hashish* or a sticky black liquid called *hash oil*.

The Use of Marijuana

Marijuana is the most common illicit drug used in the United States. After a period of decline in the last decade, its use has been increasing among young people since 2007, corresponding to a diminishing perception of the drug's risks that may be associated with increased public debate over the drug's legal status. Although the federal government considers marijuana a Schedule 1 substance (having no medicinal uses and high risk for abuse), two states have legalized marijuana for adult recreational use, and 20 states have passed laws allowing its use as a treatment for certain medical conditions.

Marijuana is usually smoked in hand-rolled cigarettes (joints) or in pipes or water pipes (bongs). It is also smoked in blunts—cigars that have been emptied of tobacco and refilled with a mixture of marijuana and tobacco. Marijuana

"DrugFacts: Marijuana," National Institute on Drug Abuse, January 2014, pp. 1–4.

smoke has a pungent and distinctive, usually sweet-and-sour, odor. Marijuana can also be mixed in food or brewed as a tea.

When marijuana is smoked, THC rapidly passes from the lungs into the bloodstream, which carries the chemical to the brain and other organs throughout the body. It is absorbed more slowly when ingested in food or drink.

Marijuana's Effect on the Brain

However it is ingested, THC acts on specific molecular targets on brain cells, called cannabinoid receptors. These receptors are ordinarily activated by chemicals similar to THC that naturally occur in the body and are part of a neural communication network called the endocannabinoid system. This system plays an important role in normal brain development and function.

Marijuana use may have a wide range of effects, particularly on cardiopulmonary and mental health.

The highest density of cannabinoid receptors is found in parts of the brain that influence pleasure, memory, thinking, concentration, sensory and time perception, and coordinated movement. Marijuana overactivates the endocannabinoid system, causing the "high" and other effects that users experience. These effects include altered perceptions and mood, impaired coordination, difficulty with thinking and problem solving, and disrupted learning and memory.

Marijuana also affects brain development, and when it is used heavily by young people, its effects on thinking and memory may last a long time or even be permanent. A recent study of marijuana users who began using in adolescence revealed substantially reduced connectivity among brain areas responsible for learning and memory. And a large long-term study in New Zealand showed that people who began smoking marijuana heavily in their teens lost an average of 8 points in IQ between age 13 and age 38. Importantly, the lost cognitive abilities were not fully restored in those who quit smoking marijuana as adults. Those who started smoking marijuana in adulthood did not show significant IQ declines.

The Cardiopulmonary Effects of Marijuana

Marijuana use may have a wide range of effects, particularly on cardiopulmonary and mental health.

Marijuana smoke is an irritant to the lungs, and frequent marijuana smokers can have many of the same respiratory problems experienced by tobacco smokers, such as daily cough and phlegm production, more frequent acute chest illness, and a heightened risk of lung infections. One study found that people who smoke marijuana frequently but do not smoke tobacco have more health problems and miss more days of work than those who don't smoke marijuana, mainly because of respiratory illnesses. It is not yet known whether marijuana smoking contributes to risk for lung cancer.

A recent analysis of data from several studies found that marijuana use more than doubles a driver's risk of being in an accident.

Marijuana also raises heart rate by 20–100 percent shortly after smoking; this effect can last up to 3 hours. In one study, it was estimated that marijuana users have a 4.8-fold increase in the risk of heart attack in the first hour after smoking the drug. This risk may be greater in older individuals or in those with cardiac vulnerabilities.

Marijuana and Mental Illness

A number of studies have linked chronic marijuana use and mental illness. High doses of marijuana can produce a temporary psychotic reaction (involving hallucinations and paranoia) in some users, and using marijuana can worsen the course of illness in patients with schizophrenia. A series of large studies following users across time also showed a link between marijuana use and later development of psychosis. This relationship was influenced by genetic variables as well as the amount of drug used, drug potency, and the age at which it was first taken—those who start young are at increased risk for later problems.

Associations have also been found between marijuana use and other mental health problems, such as depression, anxiety, suicidal thoughts among adolescents, and personality disturbances, including a lack of motivation to engage in typically rewarding activities. More research is still needed to confirm and better understand these linkages.

Marijuana use during pregnancy is associated with increased risk of neurobehavioral problems in babies. Because THC and other compounds in marijuana mimic the body's own endocannabinoid chemicals, marijuana use by pregnant mothers may alter the developing endocannabinoid system in the brain of the fetus. Consequences for the child may include problems with attention, memory, and problem solving.

Additionally, because it seriously impairs judgment and motor coordination, marijuana contributes to risk of injury or death while driving a car. A recent analysis of data from several studies found that marijuana use more than doubles a driver's risk of being in an accident. The combination of marijuana and alcohol is worse than either substance alone with respect to driving impairment.

The Addictiveness of Marijuana

Contrary to common belief, marijuana is addictive. Estimates from research suggest that about 9 percent of users become addicted to marijuana; this number increases among those who start young (to about 17 percent, or 1 in 6) and among people who use marijuana daily (to 25–50 percent).

Long-term marijuana users trying to quit report withdrawal symptoms including irritability, sleeplessness, decreased appetite, anxiety, and drug craving, all of which can make it difficult to abstain. Behavioral interventions, including cognitive-behavioral therapy and motivational incentives (i.e., providing vouchers for goods or services to patients who remain abstinent) have proven to be effective in treating marijuana addiction. Although no medications are currently available, recent discoveries about the workings of the endocannabinoid system offer promise for the development of medications to ease withdrawal, block the intoxicating effects of marijuana, and prevent relapse.

Drug Use Negatively Impacts Health, Productivity, and Crime

United Nations Office on Drugs and Crime

The United Nations Office on Drugs and Crime operates in all regions of the world through an extensive network of field offices to fight against illicit drugs and international crime.

The key impact of illicit drug use on society is the negative health consequences experienced by members of society. Drug use can have a serious health impact, even for casual users. Cocaine can induce a stroke; amphetamines can induce lethal arrhythmias or hyperthermia upon first exposure. The use of cannabis may seriously impair the user's driving capacity. Chronic cannabis use can lead to drug dependency as well as a number of behavioural and psychiatric conditions, including internalizing disorders such as anxiety or depression. Indirect impacts include increased prevalence of infectious diseases among drug users as well as cardiovascular dysfunctions, lung diseases, kidney function impairments and endocrine dysfunctions.

The Health Impact of Drugs

Drug control tends to reduce the number of users, and thus the overall negative health impact on society. For the remaining user population, potential negative side effects of the existence of a black market may include a higher risk of obtaining low-quality drugs as traffickers attempt to increase their profits by "cutting" the substances with diluents to make more doses. In some countries, the fear of evoking a criminal justice

"Impact on Society and State," World Drug Report 2012, United Nations Office On Drugs and Crime, June 2012, pp. 69–71. Copyright © 2012 by World Drug Report 2012. All rights reserved. Reproduced by permission.

system response and of harsh enforcement measures may deter drug users from seeking treatment or other medical attention.

Drug-related deaths—whether by overdose, drug-induced accident, suicide or medical conditions associated with or exacerbated by illicit drugs—represent the most severe health consequence of drug use. Some 0.2 million people die from drug use every year. Approximately half of those cases involve fatal overdoses. Moreover, drug-related deaths often affect young people. In Europe, for example, the mean age for deaths stemming from overdose is the mid-30s.

Drug use, notably injecting drug use, is also a significant vector for spreading HIV and hepatitis B and C. Of the estimated 16 million injecting drug users worldwide, UNODC [United Nations Office on Drugs and Crime] estimates that almost one in five is HIV-positive. Approximately the same proportion are infected with hepatitis B, whereas some 8 million—about half of all injecting drug users—are infected with hepatitis C. These viruses can cause or exacerbate a range of symptoms and ailments, with a potentially fatal outcome.

While in 2010 some 7.9 million people in the United States alone needed treatment for problems related to illicit drug use, only 2.2 million received it.

UNODC estimates suggest that about 12 per cent of illicit drug users—the cohort of people who report having used an illicit drug at least once in the past year—develop drug dependency and become "problem" drug users. This proportion varies greatly between different drugs. Data from the 2010 United States household survey on drug use and health, for instance, suggest that 15 per cent of cocaine users can be considered to be substance-dependent. This proportion rises to 26 per cent for methamphetamine and to more than 50 per cent for heroin. For cannabis, the proportion is 10 per cent.

Drug-dependent persons require treatment, which may place a financial burden on the individuals and their families, or on society at large. In 2009, some 4.5 million people worldwide were receiving treatment for problems related to illicit drug use; among these, about 1 million were Europeans (excluding Belarusians, Moldovans, Russians and Ukrainians). In the United States, 2 million people received such treatment in 2002. In the same year, the health-related costs of illicit drug use in that country were estimated at $15.8 billion, equivalent to 0.15 per cent of GDP [gross domestic product]. Assuming that the health costs develop proportionally to the number of persons in treatment and that health cost increases are in line with nominal GDP growth, annual drug-related health costs in the United States may have increased to some $24 billion by 2010. Somewhat lower expenditure levels have been reported from other Western countries.

While in 2010 some 7.9 million people in the United States alone needed treatment for problems related to illicit drug use, only 2.2 million received it. At the global level, the ratio is less than one in five, according to UNODC estimates. Expressed in monetary terms, at current prevalence rates (number of users), some $200 billion–250 billion (0.3–0.4 per cent of global GDP) would have been needed to cover global costs related to treatment for illicit drug use in 2010.

The Impact on Productivity

Although many studies suggest that the impact of illicit drug use on a society's productivity—in purely monetary terms—may be far more significant than the health impact, it is less commonly discussed. Productivity may decline owing to a large number of factors, including absenteeism, workplace accidents and conflicts at the workplace, to name just a few.

A 2011 study estimated productivity losses in the United States at $120 billion (0.9 per cent of GDP) for the year 2007. This is significantly higher than the health-related costs of illicit drug use discussed above and would be equivalent to 62 per cent of all drug-related costs (calculated using a cost-of-illness approach). Reduced labour participation and incarcerations were the main causes. A similar study undertaken in Canada in 2002 suggested that productivity losses due to illicit drug use amounted to 4.7 billion Canadian dollars (0.4 per cent of GDP). Moreover, in Australia, a study found that the cost of such productivity losses amounted to 2.1 billion Australian dollars for the financial year 2004/05 (0.3 per cent of GDP). These costs are four and eight times higher than the health-related costs, respectively.

In contrast to health costs, productivity loss calculations try to value the loss of potential resources. Productivity losses represent work that was never performed, but could reasonably be expected to have been performed without the impact of illicit drug use. Productivity losses can be thought of as a loss of potential income and thus of GDP brought about by a reduction in the supply and/or effectiveness of the labour force.

[A US study estimates] a potential productivity loss of slightly more than $1 million for each drug-related death.

Valuations of the loss of a drug user from productive activities is typically based on the expected value of the productivity of the person who illicitly uses drugs. In the labour market, this may equal their expected earnings. Non-market or household productivity is also valued; it is equal to the cost of hiring someone to perform the services that the drug user is unable to perform because of sickness, disability or death.

The Value of Life

One key challenge for research in this area is to calculate the "value of life" of a drug user. Two of the main approaches used in the literature are the human capital approach and the demographic approach.

The United States and Canadian studies cited above use the human capital approach, in which premature deaths—a significant component of productivity losses—are valuated as the expected lifetime productivity of the deceased persons. This means that the expected salaries, including fringe benefits, of drug users until the normal retirement age are summed up, then discounted at a predetermined rate (real interest rate of 3 per cent in the United States example). Individuals who die earlier in their (potentially) productive life are given a higher value in these calculations than those closer to the age of retirement. On average, the United States estimates resulted in a potential productivity loss of slightly more than $1 million for each drug-related death.

The Australian study uses the demographic approach, which compares the actual population size and structure to the size and structure of a hypothetical alternative population free of drug use. The actual and hypothetical outputs are then compared in order to estimate the productivity losses.

The key difference between these approaches is that the human capital approach calculates present and futures income flows that will no longer accrue owing to drug-related deaths in the current year. The demographic approach calculates the income flows that would have accrued in the absence of drug-related deaths in the current and previous years.

The Impact on Crime

Illicit drug use is also closely linked to crime, in various ways. Drug users often resort to acquisitive crime to finance their habit. Additionally, many criminals are under the influence of illicit drugs, which reduce inhibitions, when committing crime. Illicit drug use is frequently associated with behavioural problems, which, depending on the substance and the amounts used, may include or result in aggression or violence. That said, drug users may have been affected by conduct disorders and anti-social personality disorders prior to their drug use, which makes them susceptible to involvement in crime and drug abuse.

As a result, criminals in general tend to show far higher levels of drug use than the rest of the population. Urine tests made in 10 major cities in the United States in 2010 revealed that, on average, about 70 per cent of the arrested males had used an illicit drug in comparison to a rate of current drug use among the general male population of 11.2 per cent. Similar results were found in Australia, where one study, based on information collected from 10 sites throughout the country, found that 65 per cent of all detainees, including drug offenders, tested positive for illicit drugs in 2008. In the United Kingdom, results in the same range were found for England and Wales as well.

The costs of drug-related crime can be substantial. In the United Kingdom, a study of the economic and social costs of illicit drug use suggested that the cost of drug-related crime (mainly fraud, burglary, robbery and shoplifting) in England and Wales totalled some £13.9 billion in 2003/04, equivalent to 90 per cent of all social and economic costs related to drug abuse.

Similarly, a study undertaken in Austria estimated the costs of crime related to illicit drug use (mainly fraud, robbery, burglary, car theft, other theft and extortion) at €2.6 billion for the year 2002, which is equivalent to 80 per cent of the total social costs caused by drug use. The costs to the general public of these drug-related crimes were found to be more than eight times larger than the benefits drug users obtained by selling the stolen goods.

Crime and drugs are also linked through drug trafficking. While traffickers generally avoid attracting attention from law enforcement authorities, at times competition between different trafficking groups can generate violence, often including homicide, as the different groups fight to defend or increase their illicit market shares. Moreover, criminal groups with access to large drug profits also often use them for corruption, which may with time lead to significant erosion of the State's authority as drug criminals buy themselves impunity.

Methamphetamine and Other Drugs Are Not as Dangerous as Alleged

Carl Hart, interviewed by Reason.com

Carl Hart is associate professor of psychology and psychiatry at Columbia University in New York.

"We haven't had an adult conversation about drugs in America," says neuroscientist Carl Hart. The Columbia University academic, known for his experiments tracking the brain activity of drug users, is trying to rectify that state of affairs with his new book, *High Price: A Neuroscientist's Journey of Self-Discovery That Challenges Everything You Know About Drugs and Society.*

An Interview with a Neuroscientist

Hart, an associate professor of psychology, has both a personal and professional perspective on drugs. A former user and dealer, he's a featured character in Eugene Jarecki's anti-drug war documentary *The House I Live In*, which explores, among other things, Hart's relationship with his son Tobias, who recently served time on a drug charge. Hart's new book, which makes a case for decriminalization, is both a memoir and an exploration of the latest neuroscientific research on drug use.

Hart spoke at *Reason*'s Los Angeles office in June about meth, math, violence, and what science can tell us about drug policy. . . .

Carl Hart: This book is a hybrid of memoir, science book, and policy. What I'd like to talk about is the science that I've been doing and that other people have been doing with methamphetamine.

Back in 2005 I got a call from the Office of National Drug Control Policy asking me to participate in a roundtable of writers who were interested in writing stories about methamphetamine. They wanted their stories to be more realistic— they were writers for things like *Law and Order, CSI*, magazines, and so forth. At this roundtable the panelists were a U.S. assistant attorney, an undercover narcotics officer, an adult person who was addicted to methamphetamine, an adolescent who was addicted to methamphetamine, and myself. My role at the panel was to help participants understand where the science was at the time, what we knew from the empirical information.

The Effects of Methamphetamine

Basically what I said was that we had tested relatively low oral doses in the laboratory, where we evaluated the effects of those doses of methamphetamine on cognitive performance, mood, heart rate, blood pressure, those sorts of things. My conclusions were that the drug was quite unremarkable. In fact, in people who are well-rested you didn't see much in terms of cognitive disruption, or you didn't see any. Those low doses produce some euphoria, but a moderate range of euphoria.

What I'd like to do is evaluate [the] sorts of claims that seem to be pervasive in our history when it comes to drugs.

When I finished my presentation my fellow panelists were horrified. They were horrified because they had told stories about the horrors of methamphetamine that they saw in the natural ecology. They recounted stories of methamphetamine users developing superhuman strength. When someone was on methamphetamine, it was said, you had to increase the caliber of weapon; regular Tasers no longer worked with these individuals. Another story that was recounted was that methamphetamine was like no other drug that law enforcement had ever seen. This particular cop said he had more than twentysomething years experience on the force and had never seen anything like methamphetamine—and he had seen crack users and that sort of thing. This drug methamphetamine, he claimed, exerted unique pharmacological effects. Finally, when I challenged some of the claims that were being made, he turned to me and said: "Dr. Hart, when you see a parent cut the head of their child off and throw it at you then maybe perhaps you will become a believer."

I tried to explain that these types of stories, these anecdotes—particularly about drugs—weren't new. We had heard them before. The stories about drug users developing superhuman strength, the stories about some new drug being like no other drug we've ever seen, and the stories about drugs causing this sort of wide range of cognitive disruption.

What I'd like to do is evaluate these three sorts of claims that seem to be pervasive in our history when it comes to drugs.

The Myth of Superhuman Strength

The first [is] these individuals developing superhuman strength. If you go back to *The New York Times*, for example, on February 8, 1914, what you find is a huge editorial: "Negro Cocaine Fiends Are New Southern Menace." In this piece the author argued that black people, when they have cocaine, they develop superhuman strength. So much so that southern police forces had to increase the caliber of their weapons. They moved from the .32 caliber weapon to the .38 caliber weapon because the .32 caliber weapon or bullets didn't affect black people on cocaine.

I know it sounds comical, but this was actually believed. And these things come back in new forms. Maybe a year and a half ago, two years ago, we heard about the guy in Miami who chewed the face off of another guy. It was said that the person was on bath salts and that bath salts cause such extreme effects that you get this kind of behavior. But when the toxicology was in, there were no bath salts in this person's system. The only thing that was in the person's system was THC, and we don't know when was the last time this person used THC. It could have been weeks.

The point is that these arguments, these claims, they are recycled generation after generation. And we laugh at some of them because of the language, but the language is tempered to fit the contemporary folk. It doesn't seem so outrageous if you're not a critical thinker. But of course most of these claims are just exaggeration.

The Cognitive Effects of Methamphetamine

The [second] claim is that methamphetamine produces unique cognitive effects. What I did, along with my Ph.D. student at the time, Matt Kirkpatrick, is that we ran a study in which we gave research participants—of course we passed all of the ethical requirements—intranasal methamphetamine at a low dose and a large dose on one day. It's all under blind conditions. We also gave participants dextroamphetamine, the active ingredient in Adderall, on other days. Of course a placebo was included.

> We should rethink and reevaluate how we are regulating drugs like methamphetamine, drugs like heroin, drugs like cocaine, and so forth.

We evaluated the effects of these drugs to see whether or not methamphetamine was unique compared to just regular amphetamine, because when you look at the chemical structure of these drugs, they look almost identical excepting for the meth group, which is on the methamphetamine structure. What we found was that the drugs produced nearly identical effects. They are the same drug. Methamphetamine is the same drug as the active ingredient in Adderall. The notion that methamphetamine produces unique effects is just simply not supported by evidence.

Finally I was interested in this notion that methamphetamine causes all of these cognitive disruptions. If you all have been paying attention in the country for the past 5 to 10 years you might know something about the Montana Meth Project, in which they make these slick advertisements—which they call "education"—about the dangers of methamphetamine. Oftentimes these advertisements indicate that methamphetamine causes widespread cognitive disruptions. And it seemed as though the scientific literature was in support of what was being said in these advertisements.

In 2012, I published a review of all the scientific literature that was relevant for cognitive performance and for brain imaging. What I concluded was the interpretations in the scientific literature were wildly overstated in terms of the effects of methamphetamine on cognition, in terms of the effects of methamphetamine on brain structure. My paper was published in *Neuropsychopharmacology* in 2012.

The Need for Decriminalization and Education

So given that our drug policy is based on these faulty assumptions, one of the things that I call for in *High Price* is that we should rethink and reevaluate how we are regulating drugs like methamphetamine, drugs like heroin, drugs like cocaine, and so forth. And the main reason I call for this reevaluation is this: Each year in this country we arrest 1.5 million people for drug-related violations. More than 80 percent of them are for simple possession. If our assumptions that these drugs are so dangerous that we have to go after them with such ferocity are faulty, I think that we could decrease the blemishes that we put on people's records by decriminalizing drugs rather than the approach that we're taking.

When you call for decriminalization in this country you have to provide some education, because the country is quite ignorant about drug policy, about drugs in general. Decriminalization is not legalization. Legalization is what we're doing with alcohol. If you're 21 or older, you can purchase alcohol without fear of being prosecuted. You can sell alcohol legally. With decriminalization, you cannot sell drugs. They still remain illegal. Possession also remains illegal, but you can no longer get a criminal record from possessing a drug. Instead it would be treated like we treat traffic violations. That way we decrease the likelihood of putting blemishes on people's records and enhance the likelihood that they will be able to get jobs and contribute to society. When we think about the guys who have occupied the White House—President Obama, President Bush, President Clinton—all three of those guys used illegal drugs in their youth. If they would have been caught, they would've gotten felony charges and probably would not have been allowed to make the contributions that they have made to our country.

In many of the stories told about those drugs like marijuana in the 1930s, the demon rum, and that sort of thing, drugs serve as convenient tools to further demonize groups that we don't like.

One of the things that happens in this discussion is that experts are very comfortable talking on areas in which they have limited expertise. I'm not one of them, and I have limited expertise in markets. My expertise is the effects of drugs on people. But what I can tell you is why I favor decriminalization rather than legalization: Legalization will provide the opportunity for people to exaggerate the extent of the harms caused by drugs. I know that for a fact. Because the country is so ignorant about what drugs actually do, we should decriminalize and then have a corresponding increase in education about these drugs. Realistic education.

Since I've been talking about methamphetamine: Methamphetamine causes people to have increased heart rate, blood pressure, and so forth. The number one killer in the United States is heart disease. So if you have cardiac issues, the public health message will be blared: "Don't take methamphetamine!" Another issue is that methamphetamine is outstanding at keeping people awake. Chronic sleep loss associated with all kinds of cancers, associated with psychiatric illness, the public health message would be: "Please don't take methamphetamine near bedtime! Get sleep!" This is realistic education to help people. That's why my focus has been on decriminalization rather than legalization. I think the country's too ignorant, we haven't had an adult conversation about drugs, and I'm trying to do that with *High Price*.

The Demonization of Drugs

Reason: *Are all these stories just totally fabricated out of thin air? Because I recall way back when it was "demon weed" about marijuana and "devil rum."*

I don't want to leave you with the impression that psychoactive drugs don't have potentially powerful mind-altering effects. Because they do.

[But] in many of the stories told about those drugs like marijuana in the 1930s, the demon rum, and that sort of thing, drugs serve as convenient tools to further demonize groups that we don't like. We associated marijuana with those Mexicans who are taking jobs from the good folks in Texas. Black folks are taking jobs from white folks in the South, we don't like them. So we associate drugs that are not used widely in the society with a specific despised group.

Today it's a hell of a lot more difficult to demonize marijuana as we once did. Fast-forward to the 1980s. A number of people had used powdered cocaine. Hollywood was really supporting that industry. But there was not the same number of people using crack cocaine. So now you can say: This is a new form of cocaine. It's not the cocaine that you're using, my man. This is a new form. And so it becomes associated with these people, even though black people didn't use crack cocaine at higher rates than white folks. But certainly based on the media portrayal it was easier to get that impression.

Methamphetamine today is associated with despised groups. "Poor white trash." Gay folks. That sort of thing. A relatively small number of people use methamphetamine so you can vilify those groups. But it's a hell of a lot more difficult to vilify marijuana today.

We've given thousands of doses of these drugs, but we haven't seen any violence in the context in which we give these drugs.

The Issue of Addiction

What does the data show on addiction? Would decriminalization help that process of getting off of addiction? Or is addiction exaggerated in general?

The vast majority of people who use these substances are not addicted. Maybe 10 to 20 percent are, but 80 to 90 percent are not. Most of our attention, when we talk about these drugs, is focused on the small pathological group. I focus more on the 80 to 90 percent.

I hope that we would redistribute the money that law enforcement currently gets. We spend $26 billion a year on dealing with this drug problem. If we redistribute the money into treatment and treatment research it would enhance treatment. We currently have some pretty good treatments to treat substance abuse. It's just that we also have a lot of quacks out there.

We also have to realize that, like law enforcement, the treatment industry has a stake in our current approach. It's either jail or treatment. [But that] doesn't make any sense when the vast majority of people don't need either.

The Research on Drugs

Does the government make it difficult for people to study illegal drugs?

I sit on a number of review committees and one of the things we want to make sure before people get approval to study these drugs is that they have the appropriate amount of experience to do this research, and to make sure that they have the appropriate safeguards in place. Because you can imagine if you had people do this kind of research and they don't have the experience and they don't have the appropriate safeguards: If someone gets hurt you can imagine how that will set back the scientific investigation into this study. Think about Timothy Leary. His antics set back the research into hallucinogens 40 years. We don't want to see that happen again.

Is there any study that has ever shown that any of these substances force people to do bad things—violence, crimes, and so on?

We have been doing this research for decades in which we bring people into the lab and administer drugs in order to develop better treatments, in order to determine the effects of drugs on people for a wide range of reasons. We've given drugs like heroin, methamphetamine, crack cocaine, marijuana, you name it. Alcohol. We've given thousands of doses of these drugs, but we haven't seen any violence in the context in which we give these drugs.

That's not to say that people who use drugs don't get violent sometimes. You might see some violence with some of these drugs, but it's certainly not because of the pharmacology of the drugs. When we have this kind of discussion we sometimes think: If one person gets violent on crack cocaine, that's enough to change the policy. That's ridiculous.

The notion that we can prevent every accident, every sort of bad thing from happening in a society—if people have that notion they probably shouldn't be allowed to talk to the public.

Drug Prohibition
Is More Dangerous
than Decriminalization

David Boaz

David Boaz is the executive vice president of the Cato Institute.

Michael Gerson, former speechwriter for President George W. Bush and now a columnist for the *Washington Post*, has denounced libertarianism as "morally empty," "anti-government," "a scandal," "an idealism that strangles mercy," guilty of "selfishness," "rigid ideology," and "rigorous ideological coldness." (He's starting to repeat himself.)

An Opponent of Legalization

In his May 9 [2011] column, "Ron Paul's Land of Second-Rate Values," he went after Rep. Paul for his endorsement of drug legalization in the Republican presidential debate. "Dotty uncle," he fumed, alleging that Paul has "contempt for the vulnerable and suffering." Paul holds "second-rate values," he added.

What did Paul do to set him off? He said that adult Americans ought to have the freedom to make their own decisions about their personal lives—from how they worship, to what they eat and drink, to what drugs they use. And he mocked the paternalist mindset: "How many people here would use heroin if it were legal? I bet nobody would say, 'Oh yeah, I need the government to take care of me. I don't want to use heroin, so I need these laws.'"

Gerson accused Paul of mocking not paternalists but addicts: "Paul is not content to condemn a portion of his fellow

David Boaz, "Drug Decriminalization Has Failed? It Just Ain't So!," Freeman, September 2011, pp. 6–7. Copyright © 2011 by Freeman. All rights reserved. Reproduced by permission.

citizens to self-destruction; he must mock them in their decline." Gerson wants to treat them with compassion. But let's be clear: He thinks the compassionate way to treat suffering people is to put them in jail. And in the California case *Brown v. Plata*, the Supreme Court just reminded us what it means to hold people in prison:

> California's prisons are designed to house a population just under 80,000, but . . . the population was almost double that. The State's prisons had operated at around 200% of design capacity for at least 11 years. Prisoners are crammed into spaces neither designed nor intended to house inmates. As many as 200 prisoners may live in a gymnasium, monitored by as few as two or three correctional officers. As many as 54 prisoners may share a single toilet. Because of a shortage of treatment beds, suicidal inmates may be held for prolonged periods in telephone-booth-sized cages without toilets.

Our last three presidents have all acknowledged they used illegal drugs in their youth. Yet they don't seem to think . . . that their lives would have been made better by arrest, conviction, and incarceration.

Gerson knows this. His May 27 column quoted this very passage and concluded, "[I]t is absurd and outrageous to treat [prisoners] like animals while hoping they return to us as responsible citizens."

The Impact of Jail

Gerson contrasted the "arrogance" of Paul's libertarian approach to the approach of "a Republican presidential candidate [who] visited a rural drug treatment center outside Des Moines. Moved by the stories of recovering young addicts, Texas Gov. George W. Bush talked of his own struggles with alcohol. 'I'm on a walk. And it's a never-ending walk as far as

I'm concerned. . . . I want you to know that your life's walk is shared by a lot of other people, even some who wear suits.'"

Gerson seems to have missed the point of his anecdote. Neither Bush nor the teenagers in a Christian rehab center were sent to jail. They overcame their substance problems through faith and personal responsibility. But Gerson and Bush support the drug laws under which more than 1.5 million people a year are arrested and some 500,000 people are currently in jail.

Our last three presidents have all acknowledged they used illegal drugs in their youth. Yet they don't seem to think—nor does Gerson suggest—that their lives would have been made better by arrest, conviction, and incarceration. If libertarianism is a second-rate value, where does hypocrisy rank?

The Cost of Enforcement

Gerson seems to have a fantastical view of our world today. He writes, "[D]rug legalization fails. The de facto decriminalization of drugs in some neighborhoods—say, in Washington, D.C.—has encouraged widespread addiction."

This is mind-boggling. What has failed in Washington, D.C., is drug prohibition. As Mike Riggs of *Reason* magazine wrote, "I want to know where in D.C. one can get away with slinging or using in front of a cop. The 2,874 people arrested by the MPD [Metropolitan Police Department] for narcotics violations between Jan. 1 and April 9 of this year would probably like to know, too."

Michelle Alexander, author of *The New Jim Crow*, writes, "Crime rates have fluctuated over the past few decades—and currently are at historical lows—but imprisonment rates have soared. Quintupled. And the vast majority of that increase is due to the War on Drugs, a war waged almost exclusively in poor communities of color." Michael Gerson should ask Professor Alexander for a tour of these neighborhoods where he thinks drugs are de facto decriminalized.

In a recent Cato Institute report, Jeffrey Miron of Harvard University estimated that governments could save $41.3 billion a year if they decriminalized drugs, an indication of the resources we're putting into police, prosecutions, and prisons to enforce the war on drugs.

Drug prohibition itself creates high levels of crime. Addicts commit crimes to pay for a habit that would be easily affordable if it were legal.

The Failure of Prohibition

What Gerson correctly observes is communities wracked by crime, corruption, social breakdown, and widespread drug use. But that is a result of the failure of prohibition, not decriminalization. This is an old story. The murder rate rose with the start of alcohol Prohibition, remained high during Prohibition, and then declined for 11 consecutive years when Prohibition ended. And corruption of law enforcement became notorious.

Drug prohibition itself creates high levels of crime. Addicts commit crimes to pay for a habit that would be easily affordable if it were legal. Police sources have estimated that as much as half the property crime in some major cities is committed by drug users. More dramatically, because drugs are illegal, participants in the drug trade cannot go to court to settle disputes, whether between buyer and seller or between rival sellers. When black-market contracts are breached, the result is often some form of violent sanction.

When Gerson writes that "responsible, self-governing citizens . . . are cultivated in institutions—families, religious communities and decent, orderly neighborhoods," he should reflect on what happens to poor communities under prohibition. Drug prohibition has created a criminal subculture in our inner cities. The immense profits to be had from a black-market business make drug dealing the most lucrative endeavor for many people, especially those who care least about getting on the wrong side of the law. Drug dealers become the most visibly successful people in inner-city communities, the ones with money and clothes and cars. Social order is turned upside down when the most successful people in a community are criminals. The drug war makes peace and prosperity virtually impossible in inner cities.

There is a place where drugs have been decriminalized, not just de facto but in law. Maybe Gerson should have cited it instead of Washington, D.C. Trouble is, it doesn't make his point. Ten years ago Portugal decriminalized all drugs. Recently Glenn Greenwald studied the Portuguese experience in a study for the Cato Institute. He reported, "Portugal, whose drug problems were among the worst in Europe, now has the lowest usage rate for marijuana and one of the lowest for cocaine. Drug-related pathologies, including HIV transmission, hepatitis transmission and drug-related deaths, have declined significantly."

Drug decriminalization fails? It just ain't so.

CHAPTER 3

| Should Marijuana
Be Legalized?

Overview: For First Time, Americans Favor Legalizing Marijuana

Art Swift

Art Swift is managing editor for Gallup, a research company.

For marijuana advocates, the last 12 months have been a period of unprecedented success as Washington and Colorado became the first states to legalize recreational use of marijuana. And now for the first time, a clear majority of Americans (58%) say the drug should be legalized. This is in sharp contrast to the time Gallup first asked the question in 1969, when only 12% favored legalization.

Public support for legalization more than doubled in the 1970s, growing to 28%. It then plateaued during the 1980s and 1990s before inching steadily higher since 2000, reaching 50% in 2011.

A sizable percentage of Americans (38%) this year admitted to having tried the drug, which may be a contributing factor to greater acceptance.

Success at the ballot box in the past year in Colorado and Washington may have increased Americans' tolerance for marijuana legalization. Support for legalization has jumped 10 percentage points since last November and the legal momentum shows no sign of abating. Last week, California's second-highest elected official, Lt. Gov. Gavin Newsom, said that pot should be legal in the Golden State, and advocates of legalization are poised to introduce a statewide referendum in 2014 to legalize the drug.

The Obama administration has also been flexible on the matter. Despite maintaining the government's firm opposition to legalizing marijuana under federal law, in late August Deputy Attorney General James Cole announced the Justice Department would not challenge the legality of Colorado's and Washington's successful referendums, provided that those states maintain strict rules regarding the drug's sale and distribution.

Americans 65 and older are the only age group that still opposes legalizing marijuana.

The movement to legalize marijuana mirrors the relatively recent success of the movement to legalize gay marriage, which voters have also approved now in 14 states. Public support for gay marriage, which Americans also overwhelmingly opposed in the past, has increased dramatically, reaching majority support in the last two years.

Independents Fueling Growth in Acceptance of Legalizing Marijuana

Independents' growing support for legalization has mostly driven the jump in Americans' overall support. Sixty-two percent of independents now favor legalization, up 12 points from November 2012. Support for legalization among Democrats and Republicans saw little change. Yet there is a marked divide between Republicans, who still oppose legalizing marijuana, and Democrats and independents.

Young Adults More Likely to Support Legalization

Americans 65 and older are the only age group that still opposes legalizing marijuana. Still, support among this group has jumped 14 percentage points since 2011.

In contrast, 67% of Americans aged 18 to 29 back legalization. Clear majorities of Americans aged 30 to 64 also favor legalization.

Bottom Line

It has been a long path toward majority acceptance of marijuana over the past 44 years, but Americans' support for legalization accelerated as the new millennium began. This acceptance of a substance that most people might have considered forbidden in the late 1960s and 1970s may be attributed to changing social mores and growing social acceptance. The increasing prevalence of medical marijuana as a socially acceptable way to alleviate symptoms of diseases such as arthritis, and as a way to mitigate side effects of chemotherapy, may have also contributed to Americans' growing support.

Whatever the reasons for Americans' greater acceptance of marijuana, it is likely that this momentum will spur further legalization efforts across the United States. Advocates of legalizing marijuana say taxing and regulating the drug could be financially beneficial to states and municipalities nationwide. But detractors such as law enforcement and substance abuse professionals have cited health risks including an increased heart rate, and respiratory and memory problems.

With Americans' support for legalization quadrupling since 1969, and localities on the East Coast such as Portland, Maine, considering a symbolic referendum to legalize marijuana, it is clear that interest in this drug and these issues will remain elevated in the foreseeable future.

The War on Marijuana Targets Individuals of Color

American Civil Liberties Union

The American Civil Liberties Union (ACLU) is a national organization advocating for individual rights and liberties guaranteed by the US Constitution and US laws.

The most effective way to eliminate arrests for marijuana use and possession, the racial disparities among such arrests, and the Fourth Amendment violations that often accompany such arrests, is to legalize marijuana. For instance, in Washington, Blacks were almost three times more likely to be arrested for marijuana possession as whites, and the Black/white racial disparity in marijuana possession arrests increased by 42% between 2001 and 2010. By passing Initiative 502, which legalized possession of marijuana for people 21 years or older and thus ended arrests of adults for possession, Washington has also ended such racial disparities with respect to marijuana possession arrests of people 21 years or older.

Legalize Marijuana Use and Possession

Marijuana legalization should occur through a system of taxation, licensing, and regulation under which private businesses licensed and regulated by the state can sell marijuana subject to a sales tax. Legalization through taxing and licensing would not only solve the arrests epidemic and its attendant racial disparities by removing marijuana possession and use from the criminal justice system, it would also save cash-strapped state and local governments millions of dollars in decreased police, jail, and court costs that could be redirected to supporting public health approaches to drug addiction and confronting more serious crime. For example, in 2010, 61% of all drug arrests in Colorado were for marijuana possession, the ninth highest percentage share in the country. Following passage of Amendment 64, which legalized marijuana possession for adults, police can reinvest those resources toward other more important public health and safety objectives. At the same time, legalization through taxation and regulation would raise new revenue that states could apportion to public schools, substance abuse prevention, including community- and school-based programs, as well as to general funds, local budgets, research and health care.

States should ... license, tax, and regulate marijuana production, distribution, and possession for persons 21 or older.

The legalization of marijuana will also provide more seriously ill patients with critical access to a medicine that can alleviate their pain and suffering without the harmful side effects—such as nausea or loss of appetite—of many prescription medicines. Currently there are 19 states, along with the District of Columbia, that allow marijuana for medicinal purposes.

Legalization would also reduce the demand for marijuana from Mexico, thereby removing the profit incentives of the Mexican marijuana trade and reducing its associated violence. Indeed, one study estimates that the marijuana legalization laws in Colorado and Washington will deprive Mexican drug cartels of $1.425 and $1.372 billion in profits, respectively.

Therefore, states should:

- License, tax, and regulate marijuana production, distribution, and possession for persons 21 or older.

- Remove criminal and civil penalties for activities so authorized.

- Tax marijuana sales.

- Earmark marijuana-related revenues to public schools and substance-abuse prevention, including community- and school-based programs, as well as general funds, local budgets, research and health care.

The specific contours of regulation will vary from jurisdiction to jurisdiction, depending on local laws and public opinion. For instance, in Washington, Initiative 502 prohibits home growing of marijuana except for medical marijuana patients, whereas in Colorado, home growing is permitted. Therefore, this report offers examples of regulations for potential consideration as opposed to endorsing a fixed set of rules for every jurisdiction. Initiative 502 in Washington provides one regulatory model: it ensures that establishments licensed to sell marijuana are located at least 1,000 feet from schools, playgrounds, and parks, and do not display marijuana in a way that is visible to the public; limits availability to stores that sell no products other than marijuana; prohibits public use and display of marijuana; prohibits sales to minors; restricts advertising generally and bans advertising in places frequented by youth; and establishes a standard for driving under the influence [DUI] of marijuana (i.e., active THC content) that would operate like the alcohol DUI standards. State agencies can also regulate the numbers of stores per county, operating hours, security, quality control, labeling, and other health and safety issues.

Marijuana legalization through a tax and regulate system should not mandate state employees to grow, distribute, or sell marijuana, as such conduct would require state officials to violate federal law and thus likely be preempted by federal law (the Controlled Substances Act, 21 U.S.C. §801) as it now stands. But legalization laws can require state officials to perform administrative, ministerial, and regulatory duties necessary to implement and oversee state laws and regulations.

Depenalization not only removes marijuana possession and use from the grasp of the criminal justice system, it avoids the pitfalls associated with replacing criminal penalties with civil penalties.

As a society, we permit the controlled use of alcohol and tobacco, substances that are dangerous to health and at times to public safety. We educate society about those dangers, and have constructed a system of laws that allow for the use and possession of these substances while seeking to protect the public from their dangers. There is no reason, particularly given the findings of this report, that such a system cannot and should not also be constructed for marijuana use and possession.

Depenalize Marijuana Use and Possession

If legalizing marijuana through taxation and licensing is unobtainable, states can take significant steps toward reducing marijuana arrests and their damaging consequences by removing all criminal and civil penalties for marijuana use and possession. Under depenalization, there would be no arrests, prosecutions, tickets, or fines for marijuana use or possession, as long as such use and possession complied with any existing regulations governing such activity.

Depenalization not only removes marijuana possession and use from the grasp of the criminal justice system, it avoids the pitfalls associated with replacing criminal penalties with civil penalties.

Therefore, states should:

- Amend their current criminal and civil statutes to remove all penalties for persons 21 or older for possession of marijuana for personal use (the amount could be, for example, limited to an ounce or less, but this can be determined on a state by state basis).

Decriminalize Marijuana Use and Possession

If both legalizing marijuana use and possession through taxation and regulation and depenalization are unobtainable, states can take steps toward reducing marijuana arrests by decriminalizing marijuana possession for adults and youth. Decriminalization replaces all criminal penalties for marijuana use and possession with civil penalties. Massachusetts provides a useful case study on the impact that decriminalization can have on reducing marijuana arrests. In 2009, Massachusetts decriminalized adult possession of an ounce or less of marijuana for personal use, with a maximum civil penalty of a $100 fine and forfeiture of the marijuana (anyone under 18 must also complete a drug awareness program). In 2008, the year before decriminalization took effect, Massachusetts arrested 8,502 people for marijuana possession; in 2009, that figure dropped to 1,240—an 85% decrease—and dropped again to 1,181 in 2010. Indeed, the arrest rate for marijuana possession in Massachusetts (18 per 100,000) is the lowest in the country. Despite being one of the 15 most populous states, in 2010 Massachusetts made the third fewest total marijuana possession arrests nationwide behind only North Dakota and Vermont. Not surprisingly, marijuana arrests now make up less than 10% of all of drug arrests in Massachusetts, by far the smallest percentage of any state in the country. Although the racial disparities in marijuana possession arrests did not improve—in fact, they grew worse: the arrest rate in 2010 was 61 per 100,000 Blacks and 16 per 100,000 whites, a ratio of 3.81—the actual number of Blacks arrested declined 83% between 2008 and 2010 (while the number of whites arrested dropped 87%).

Although reclassification of marijuana possession and use from a criminal to a civil offense is a far better alternative to the criminalization of marijuana possession, it is important to recognize that replacing marijuana possession arrests with fees, fines, and/or tickets is not an ideal solution for a number of reasons. First, the same racial disparities that exist nationwide in arrests for marijuana possession would likely be replicated in citations for civil offenses for marijuana possession. Second, the monetary fines that accompany civil offenses can place a substantial burden on those fined, particularly the young and/or poor, groups that are disproportionately targeted by police.

Third, individuals who are unable to make payments in a timely fashion, or at all, or who do not appear in court to answer to the civil charge, are subject to arrest—often by a warrant squad—which results in individuals being brought to court, and in some cases jailed, for failing to pay the fines or to appear. In addition to placing significant personal and financial burdens on the individual, this also imposes significant costs on the state, possibly exceeding the original fine imposed. Therefore, at the very least, whenever anyone is unable to pay a fine levied for marijuana possession or use, there should be alternatives to cash payments. Further, under no circumstances should the state be permitted to detain or incarcerate anyone as a penalty for failure to pay a civil fine for possessing marijuana. Fourth, allowing cities and counties to generate revenue through civil fines provides an incentive for police to enforce such civil laws aggressively.

If legalization and depenalization are unobtainable, states should:

- Amend their current criminal statutes so that possession of an ounce or less of marijuana for personal use by adults and youth would be a civil offense only, for which the maximum penalty is a small fine, with alternative penalties available for people unable to pay.

- Earmark revenues generated from marijuana-related civil penalties to public schools, substance abuse prevention, including community- and school-based programs, as well as to general funds, local budgets, research and health care.

Marijuana Should Be Legalized and Not Just Decriminalized

Drug Policy Alliance

The Drug Policy Alliance is an organization that promotes drug policies that are grounded in science, compassion, health, and human rights.

Marijuana prohibition has been a costly failure. In 2012, there were 749,825 marijuana arrests in the U.S.—nearly half of all drug arrests. More than 87 percent were for simple possession, not sale or manufacture. There are more arrests for marijuana possession every year than for all violent crimes combined. Yet marijuana is the most widely used illegal drug in the U.S. and the world. More than 110 million Americans—almost 43 percent of U.S. residents surveyed—admit to having tried marijuana at least once in their lives, and 18 million to having used it in the past month.

A Trend Away from Prohibition

Marijuana arrests also disproportionately affect young people of color. Whites reportedly consume and sell marijuana at the same rates as (or higher than) blacks and Latinos. Yet blacks and Latinos are arrested for possessing or selling marijuana at vastly disproportionate rates. In fact, blacks were nearly four times more likely to be arrested for possession than whites in 2010.

Prohibition empowers criminal organizations and contributes to violence, crime and corruption on a massive scale—

from U.S. street corners to places like Mexico, where more than 100,000 people have been killed since 2006 in the country's drug war.

Eighteen states and Washington D.C. have enacted various forms of marijuana decriminalization or legalization. Decriminalization is commonly defined as the reduction or elimination of criminal penalties for minor marijuana possession. Many of these states have replaced criminal sanctions with the imposition of civil, fine-only penalties; others have reduced marijuana possession from a felony to a fine-only misdemeanor.

Under decriminalization, marijuana possession arrests may continue, or even increase, because police may be more inclined to make arrests if they present less administrative burdens.

Evidence from states and countries that have reduced penalties not only shows no increase in marijuana or other drug use, but also substantial reductions in misdemeanor arrests where decriminalization has been implemented effectively. In 2011, California reclassified marijuana possession as an infraction (administrative violation) instead of a misdemeanor, leading to "a significant decline in misdemeanor marijuana arrests," which plunged from 54,849 in 2010 to 7,764 in 2011, and remained constant in 2012 at 7,768—a decrease of more than 80 percent. Overall drug arrests declined from 129,182 in 2010 to between 75,000 and 80,000 in 2011 and 2012.

The Problem with Decriminalization

Despite its benefits, decriminalization falls short in many ways—largely because it still lies within the framework of *prohibition*. Consequently, decriminalization still suffers from the inherent harms of prohibition—namely, an illegal, unregulated market; the unequal application of the laws (regardless of severity of penalty) toward certain groups, especially people of color; unregulated products of unknown potency and quality; and the potential for continued arrests as part of a "net-widening" phenomenon.

Under decriminalization, marijuana possession arrests may continue, or even increase, because police may be more inclined to make arrests if they present less administrative burdens as infractions, civil offenses, or even misdemeanors (without jail), as opposed to felonies. A similar process of "net-widening" occurred in parts of Australia that decriminalized marijuana, where the number of people arrested (but not booked) actually increased. Because many could not afford to pay the fines imposed after an arrest, the end result was [according to Peter Reuter] "an increase in the number of individuals being incarcerated for marijuana offenses, albeit now indirectly for their failure to pay a fine."

A misdemeanor conviction, moreover, can seriously hinder an individual's ability to succeed and participate in society by preventing him or her from obtaining employment, housing and student loans. Even an arrest record can be an obstacle to opportunities for otherwise law-abiding individuals.

Additionally, not *all* decriminalization schemes protect *all* people from risk of arrest. Even in many of the states that have reduced penalties, marijuana possession is not fully "decriminalized." Some states have defined simple marijuana possession as only one-half ounce or even less; possession of more than these amounts may still trigger harsh criminal penalties. Some states have only decriminalized a first offense, while subsequent offenses are punished severely. Other states' laws have loopholes, such as New York's, in which personal possession is formally decriminalized, but possession in "public view" remains a crime; as a result, the NYPD [New York Police Department] still arrested roughly 40,000 people in 2012—86 percent of whom were blacks and Latinos.

The Problem with Continued Prohibition

Decriminalization will also do nothing to eliminate the lucrative underground market for marijuana, estimated to be worth $30 billion or more in the U.S. This immense market is completely untaxed, a source of revenue that federal and state governments can ill-afford to neglect.

Legal regulation is not a step into the unknown—we have more than a century of experience in legally regulating thousands of different drugs.

Instead, prohibition ensures that this vast market enriches criminal organizations and produces massive violence, crime and corruption. Virtually all marijuana-related violence is the result of prohibition, which keeps responsible businesses out of the market. Illegal businesses have no legitimate means to settle disputes, so violence inevitably results—as it did during alcohol Prohibition.

The effect has been unending bloodshed in countries like Mexico, where at least 100,000 people have been killed in prohibition-related violence since late 2006. Marijuana prohibition is a major cause of this carnage; in fact, one scholar [Reuter] recently argued, "Perhaps the most serious harms [of marijuana] relate to its trafficking and production in Mexico. . . . It has caused great harm to Mexico, as a source of both homicides and corruption."

The federal government has asserted that "[M]arijuana distribution in the United States remains the single largest source of revenue for the Mexican cartels," and is "a cash crop that finances corruption and the carnage of violence year after year." Recent estimates by RAND Corporation and the Mexican Institute for Competitiveness project that legalizing marijuana nationally could reduce cartels' drug export revenues by between one-fifth and one-third.

Marijuana Taxation and Regulation

Legal regulation is not a step into the unknown—we have more than a century of experience in legally regulating thousands of different drugs. Legal regulation means common-sense controls—marijuana wouldn't be treated like Coca-Cola, available to anyone of any age, anywhere, at any time. Under most regulatory proposals, it would be taxed and regulated in a manner similar to alcoholic beverages, with age limits, licensing requirements, quality controls, and other regulatory restrictions. Just as cities, counties and states vary in the way they regulate alcohol, the same could be true for marijuana.

Revenue from taxation of marijuana sales could reach up to $8.7 billion per year if taxed like alcohol or tobacco—on top of billions in saved law enforcement resources.

In November of 2012, residents of Colorado and Washington took the historic step of rejecting the failed policy of marijuana prohibition by deciding to permit the legal regulation of marijuana sales, cultivation and distribution for adults 21 and older. In Colorado, Amendment 64 won with 54.8 percent of the vote. In Washington State, Initiative 502 won with 55.7 percent of the vote. Both states have completely eliminated all penalties for personal marijuana possession by adults; Colorado also allows adults to cultivate six marijuana plants. These states determined that simply eliminating criminal penalties for possession was not enough. Both have established regulations for the cultivation, distribution and sale of marijuana to adults. On January 1, 2014, legal marijuana sales began in Colorado—with more than $5 million in sales generated in the first week alone.

Legislators in several states have introduced (or pledged to introduce) bills to legalize marijuana. In Congress, a bipartisan group of legislators has introduced historic legislation to end federal marijuana prohibition. Internationally, Uruguay recently became the first country in the world to legalize and regulate the marijuana trade. Additional legalization proposals are under consideration in several other countries.

Revenue from taxation of marijuana sales could reach up to $8.7 billion per year if taxed like alcohol or tobacco—on top of billions in saved law enforcement resources. The New York City Comptroller's Office recently estimated "the total fiscal impact of legalizing marijuana in New York City at roughly $431 million annually." A cost-benefit analysis of regulating marijuana in England and Wales estimated "overall net external benefits in the range £0.5–1.25 billion."

The Federal Government's New Policy

In August of 2013, the Department of Justice (DOJ) announced that it will allow states to legally regulate the production, distribution, and sale of marijuana. The DOJ issued a directive to U.S. Attorneys, outlining federal priorities for enforcing marijuana laws in states that have legalized. While reserving its right to challenge state laws and enforce federal marijuana laws under certain circumstances, the directive states that the federal government will coordinate with states, rather than seek to interfere, unless states fail to meet certain federal priorities, such as preventing access by minors, diversion of marijuana, increases in violence or drugged driving, or damage to public lands.

In its memo, the DOJ openly acknowledged the many benefits of legal regulation:

> [S]trong and effective regulatory and enforcement systems to control the cultivation, distribution, sale, and possession of marijuana ... may affirmatively address [federal] priorities by, for example ... prevent[ing] diversion of marijuana outside of the regulated system and to other states, prohibiting access to marijuana by minors, and replacing an illicit

marijuana trade that funds criminal enterprises with a tightly regulated market in which revenues are tracked and accounted for.

The administration's new policy is consistent with the will of the people of Colorado and Washington, as well a substantial majority of American voters, who strongly oppose federal intervention in these states.

Indeed, public support for making marijuana legal has shifted dramatically in the last two decades, with recent polls showing greater than majority support nationwide. A recent Gallup poll found that 58 percent support legalization—a 10 percent increase over the previous year, and the highest levels of support since Gallup began asking the question more than 40 years ago.

Medical Marijuana Should Be Legalized

Marijuana Policy Project

The Marijuana Policy Project is an organization that aims to change US and state laws to eliminate prohibition of medical and nonmedical use of marijuana.

For thousands of years, marijuana has been used to treat a wide variety of ailments. Until 1937, marijuana (Cannabis sativa L.) was legal in the United States for all purposes. Presently, federal law allows only four Americans to use marijuana as a medicine.

On March 17, 1999, the National Academy of Sciences' Institute of Medicine (IOM) concluded that "there are some limited circumstances in which we recommend smoking marijuana for medical uses." The IOM report, the result of two years of research that was funded by the White House drug policy office, analyzed all existing data on marijuana's therapeutic uses.

The Medical Value of Marijuana

Marijuana is one of the safest therapeutically active substances known. No one has ever died from an overdose, and it has a wide variety of therapeutic applications, including:

- Relief from nausea and appetite loss;

- Reduction of intraocular (within the eye) pressure;

- Reduction of muscle spasms; and

- Relief from chronic pain.

Marijuana is frequently beneficial in the treatment of the following conditions:

AIDS. Marijuana can reduce the nausea, vomiting, and loss of appetite caused by the ailment itself and by various AIDS medications. Observational research has found that by relieving these side effects, medical marijuana increases the ability of patients to stay on life-extending treatment.

Marijuana can stimulate the appetite and alleviate nausea and vomiting, which are common side effects of chemotherapy treatment.

HEPATITIS C. As with AIDS, marijuana can relieve the nausea and vomiting caused by treatments for hepatitis C. In a study published in the September 2006 *European Journal of Gastroenterology & Hepatology*, patients using marijuana were better able to complete their medication regimens, leading to a 300% improvement in treatment success.

GLAUCOMA. Marijuana can reduce intraocular pressure, alleviating the pain and slowing—and sometimes stopping—damage to the eyes. (Glaucoma is the leading cause of blindness in the United States. It damages vision by increasing eye pressure over time.)

CANCER. Marijuana can stimulate the appetite and alleviate nausea and vomiting, which are common side effects of chemotherapy treatment.

MULTIPLE SCLEROSIS. Marijuana can limit the muscle pain and spasticity caused by the disease, as well as relieving tremor and unsteadiness of gait. (Multiple sclerosis is the leading cause of neurological disability among young and middle-aged adults in the United States.)

EPILEPSY. Marijuana can prevent epileptic seizures in some patients.

CHRONIC PAIN. Marijuana can alleviate chronic, often debilitating pain caused by myriad disorders and injuries.

Since 2007, three published clinical trials have found that marijuana effectively relieves neuropathic pain (pain cause by nerve injury), a particularly hard to treat type of pain that afflicts millions suffering from diabetes, HIV/AIDS, multiple sclerosis, and other illnesses.

Each of these applications has been deemed legitimate by at least one court, legislature, and/or government agency in the United States.

Many patients also report that marijuana is useful for treating arthritis, migraine, menstrual cramps, alcohol and opiate addiction, and depression and other debilitating mood disorders.

Prior to 1937, at least 27 medicines containing marijuana were legally available in the United States.

Marijuana could be helpful for millions of patients in the United States. Nevertheless, other than for the four people with special permission from the federal government, medical marijuana remains illegal under federal law!

People currently suffering from any of the conditions mentioned above, for whom the legal medical options have proven unsafe or ineffective, have two options:

1. Continue to suffer without effective treatment; or

2. Illegally obtain marijuana—and risk suffering consequences directly related to its illegality, such as:

- an insufficient supply due to the prohibition-inflated price or scarcity; impure, contaminated, or chemically adulterated marijuana;

- arrests, fines, court costs, property forfeiture, incarceration, probation, and criminal records.

The History of Marijuana's Legal Status

Prior to 1937, at least 27 medicines containing marijuana were legally available in the United States. Many were made by well-known pharmaceutical firms that still exist today, such as Squibb (now Bristol-Myers Squibb) and Eli Lilly. The Marijuana Tax Act of 1937 federally prohibited marijuana. Dr. William C. Woodward of the American Medical Association opposed the Act, testifying that prohibition would ultimately prevent the medical uses of marijuana.

The Controlled Substances Act of 1970 placed all illicit and prescription drugs into five "schedules" (categories). Marijuana was placed in Schedule I, defining it as having a high potential for abuse, no currently accepted medical use in treatment in the United States, and a lack of accepted safety for use under medical supervision.

This definition simply does not apply to marijuana. Of course, at the time of the Controlled Substances Act, marijuana had been prohibited for more than three decades. Its medical uses forgotten, marijuana was considered a dangerous and addictive narcotic.

After 16 years of court battles, the DEA's chief administrative law judge ... ruled on September 6, 1988: Marijuana, in its natural form, is one of the safest therapeutically active substances known.

A substantial increase in the number of recreational users in the 1970s contributed to the rediscovery of marijuana's medical uses:

- Many scientists studied the health effects of marijuana and inadvertently discovered marijuana's medical uses in the process.

- Many who used marijuana recreationally also suffered from diseases for which marijuana is beneficial. By accident, they discovered its therapeutic value.

As the word spread, more and more patients started self-medicating with marijuana. However, marijuana's Schedule I status bars doctors from prescribing it and severely curtails research.

Many patients would never consider the idea that an illegal drug might be their best medicine.

The Struggle in Court

In 1972, a petition was submitted to the Bureau of Narcotics and Dangerous Drugs—now the Drug Enforcement Administration (DEA)—to reschedule marijuana to make it available by prescription.

After 16 years of court battles, the DEA's chief administrative law judge, Francis L. Young, ruled on September 6, 1988:

> Marijuana, in its natural form, is one of the safest therapeutically active substances known....

> ... [T]he provisions of the [Controlled Substances] Act permit and require the transfer of marijuana from Schedule I to Schedule II.

> It would be unreasonable, arbitrary and capricious for DEA to continue to stand between those sufferers and the benefits of this substance....

Marijuana's placement in Schedule II would enable doctors to prescribe it to their patients. But top DEA bureaucrats rejected Judge Young's ruling and refused to reschedule marijuana. Two appeals later, petitioners experienced their first defeat in the 22-year-old lawsuit. On February 18, 1994, the U.S. Court of Appeals (D.C. Circuit) ruled that the DEA is allowed to reject its judge's ruling and set its own criteria—enabling the DEA to keep marijuana in Schedule I.

However, Congress has the power to reschedule marijuana via legislation, regardless of the DEA's wishes.

The Compassionate Access Program

In 1975, Robert Randall, who suffered from glaucoma, was arrested for cultivating his own marijuana. He won his case by using the "medical necessity defense," forcing the government to find a way to provide him with his medicine. As a result, the Investigational New Drug (IND) compassionate access program was established, enabling some patients to receive marijuana from the government.

The program was grossly inadequate at helping the potentially millions of people who need medical marijuana. Many patients would never consider the idea that an illegal drug might be their best medicine, and most who were fortunate enough to discover marijuana's medical value did not discover the IND program. Those who did often could not find doctors willing to take on the program's arduous, bureaucratic requirements.

In 1992, in response to a flood of new applications from AIDS patients, the George H.W. Bush administration closed the program to new applicants, and pleas to reopen it were ignored by subsequent administrations. The IND program remains in operation only for the four surviving, previously approved patients.

The Support for Ending Marijuana Prohibition

There is wide support for ending the prohibition of medical marijuana among both the public and the medical community:

- Since 1996, a majority of voters in Alaska, Arizona, California, Colorado, the District of Columbia, Maine, Massachusetts, Michigan, Montana, Nevada, Oregon, and Washington state have voted in favor of ballot initiatives to remove criminal penalties for seriously ill people who grow or possess medical marijuana.

- A May 2013 Fox News poll found that 85% of Americans think "adults should be allowed to use marijuana for medical purposes if a physician prescribes it."

- Organizations supporting some form of physician-supervised access to medical marijuana include the American Academy of Family Physicians, American Nurses Association, American Public Health Association, American Academy of HIV Medicine, Epilepsy Foundation, and many others.

- A 1990 scientific survey of oncologists (cancer specialists) found that 54% of those with an opinion favored the controlled medical availability of marijuana and 44% had already suggested at least once that a patient obtain marijuana illegally.

State governments that want to allow marijuana to be sold in pharmacies have been stymied by the federal government's overriding prohibition of marijuana.

The Need to Change the Law

The federal government has no legal authority to prevent state governments from changing their laws to remove state-level penalties for medical marijuana use. Twenty-one states and the District of Columbia have already done so: Connecticut, Delaware, Hawaii, Illinois, Maryland, New Hampshire, New Jersey, New Mexico, Rhode Island, and Vermont through their legislatures, and the others by ballot initiatives. State legislatures have the authority and moral responsibility to change state law to:

- exempt seriously ill patients from state-level prosecution for medical marijuana possession and cultivation; and

- exempt doctors who recommend medical marijuana from prosecution or the denial of any right or privilege.

Even within the confines of federal law, states can enact reforms that have the practical effect of removing the fear of patients being arrested and prosecuted under state law—as well as the symbolic effect of pushing the federal government to allow doctors to prescribe marijuana.

State governments that want to allow marijuana to be sold in pharmacies have been stymied by the federal government's overriding prohibition of marijuana.

The U.S. Supreme Court's June 2005 decision in *Gonzales v. Raich* preserved state medical marijuana laws but allowed continued federal attacks on patients, even in states with such laws. While the Justice Department indicated in 2009 that it would refrain from raids where activity is clearly legal under state law, that policy change could be reversed anytime. While the Justice department indicated in 2009 that it would refrain from raids where activity is clearly legal under state law, that policy change could be reversed anytime.

Efforts to obtain FDA [US Food and Drug Administration] approval of marijuana also remain stalled. Though some small studies of marijuana have been published or are underway, the National Institute on Drug Abuse—the only legal source of marijuana for clinical research in the U.S.—has consistently made it difficult (and often nearly impossible) for researchers to obtain marijuana for their studies. At present, it is effectively impossible to do the sort of large-scale, extremely costly trials required for FDA approval.

In the meantime, patients continue to suffer. Congress has the power and the responsibility to change federal law so that seriously ill people nationwide can use medical marijuana without fear of arrest and imprisonment.

Marijuana Legalization Is a Bad Idea for the United States

Office of National Drug Control Policy

The Office of National Drug Control Policy advises the US president on drug-control issues, coordinates drug-control activities, and produces the annual National Drug Control Strategy.

Marijuana is classified as a Schedule I drug, meaning it has a high potential for abuse and no currently accepted medical use in treatment in the United States. The main active chemical in marijuana is delta-9-tetrahydrocannabinol, more commonly called THC. THC acts upon specific sites in the brain, called cannabinoid receptors, starting off a series of cellular reactions that ultimately lead to the "high" that users experience when they smoke marijuana. Some brain areas have many cannabinoid receptors; others have few or none. The highest density of cannabinoid receptors are found in parts of the brain that influence pleasure, memory, thinking, concentrating, sensory and time perception, and coordinated movement.

The Problems with Marijuana Use

Marijuana's "high" can affect these functions in a variety of ways, causing distorted perceptions, impairing coordination, causing difficulty with thinking and problem solving, and creating problems with learning and memory. Research has demonstrated that among chronic heavy users these effects on memory can last at least seven days after discontinuing use of the drug.

These aren't the only problems connected to marijuana use. Research tells us that chronic marijuana use may increase

"Answers to Frequently Asked Questions about Marijuana," Office of National Drug Control Policy.

the risk of schizophrenia in vulnerable individuals, and high doses of the drug can produce acute psychotic reactions. Researchers have also found that adolescents' long-term use of marijuana may be linked with lower IQ (as much as an 8 point drop) later in life.

We also know that marijuana affects heart and respiratory functions. In fact, one study found that marijuana users have a nearly five-fold increase in the risk of heart attack in the first hour after smoking the drug. A study of 452 marijuana smokers (but who did not smoke tobacco) and 450 non-smokers (of either marijuana or tobacco) found that people who smoke marijuana frequently but do not smoke tobacco have more health problems, including respiratory illnesses, than nonsmokers.

There are very real consequences associated with marijuana use.

All that stated, a recent study published in the *Journal of the American Medical Association (JAMA)* found that low levels of marijuana use (with no tobacco use) produced no detrimental effect in lung function among study participants. In fact, exposure led to a mild, but not clinically significant, beneficial effect—albeit among those who smoked only one joint per day. While these findings have received wide attention from the media and from advocates of marijuana legalization, it is important to consider them in the context of the extensive body of research indicating that smoking marijuana is harmful to health. Additionally, while the study did not include a sufficient number of heavy users of marijuana to confirm a detrimental effect of such use on pulmonary function, the findings suggest this possibility.

The harms of marijuana use can also manifest in users' quality of life. In one study, heavy marijuana users reported that the drug impaired several important measures of health and quality of life, including physical and mental health, cognitive abilities, social life, and career status.

The Extent of US Marijuana Use

Marijuana is the most commonly used illicit drug in the United States. In 2011 alone, more than 18 million Americans age 12 and older reported using the drug within the past month. Approximately 4.2 million people met the diagnostic criteria for abuse of or dependence on this drug. This is more than pain relievers, cocaine, tranquilizers, hallucinogens, and heroin combined.

There are very real consequences associated with marijuana use. In 2010, marijuana was involved in more than 461,000 emergency department visits nationwide. This is nearly 39 percent of all emergency department visits involving illicit drugs, and highlights the very real dangers that can accompany use of the drug.

There have been some troubling increases in the rates of marijuana use among young Americans in the recent years.

And in 2011, approximately 872,000 Americans 12 or older reported receiving treatment for marijuana use, more than any other illicit drug. Despite some viewpoints that marijuana is harmless, these figures present a sobering picture of this drug's very real and serious harms.

Marijuana places a significant strain on our health care system, and poses considerable danger to the health and safety of the users themselves, their families, and our communities. Marijuana presents a major challenge for health care providers, public safety professionals, and leaders in communities and all levels of government seeking to reduce the drug use and its consequences throughout the country. . . .

Treatment for Marijuana

Over the last two decades, treatment admissions for marijuana have increased significantly. In 1992, approximately 93,000 people were admitted to treatment with marijuana as the primary drug for which treatment was needed.

By 2010, these admissions were estimated at 353,000. Only admissions for opiate prescription drugs and methamphetamine showed greater increases over the same period of time; however, admissions for both of these drugs in 2010 were about a half or less of marijuana admissions.

This increase in admissions for marijuana coincides with a similarly sharp rise in the potency of marijuana. In 1992, the average potency (delta-9-tetrahydrocannabinol (THC) content) of marijuana seized by the government was about 3 percent. By 2009, the average potency had more than tripled to about 11 percent.

Trends in Youth Marijuana Use

While the trend over the last 10 years has been largely positive, there have been some troubling increases in the rates of marijuana use among young Americans in the recent years.

After a steady decline and flattening in the prevalence of past-month use of marijuana among youth (12 to 17 year olds) from 2002 through 2008, the rate increased from 6.7 percent in 2008 to 7.9 percent in 2011.

Other surveys show us similar trends. The *Monitoring the Future* study found that there has been an upward trend in use over the past three to five years among 10th and 12th graders. Because most drug users use marijuana either by itself or in combination with other substances, marijuana typically drives the trends in estimates of any illicit drug use. Not surprisingly, then, the trends in past-month use of marijuana mirror the trends for past-month use of any illicit drug:

- Past-month use of marijuana among 10th graders increased from 13.8% in 2008 to 17.6% in 2011.

- Past-month use of marijuana among 12th graders increased from 18.3% in 2006 to 22.6% in 2011.

- Moreover, drug use has increased among certain youth minority populations since 2008.

- Illicit drug use has increased by 43 percent among Hispanic boys and 42 percent among African American teen girls since 2008.

These data on marijuana use are of particular concern since trends in the perception of harm of smoking marijuana also have been declining over the same period of time. Prior research indicates that declines in these perceptions are predictive of increases in use.

The extent to which young people believe that marijuana or other drugs might cause them harm is an important factor influencing their use of these substances.

It is important to examine recent trends in marijuana use within the context of longer term trends. Despite some changes in survey methodology and differences from survey to survey, we can view a fairly accurate picture of youth marijuana use over the last 40 years.

- Data showed substantial increases in youth marijuana use during the 1970s, reaching a peak in the late 1970s.

- Surveys then showed significant declines throughout the 1980s until about 1992, when rates reached a low point.

- Data showed increasing rates of marijuana use during the early to mid-1990s, reaching a peak in the late 1990s (albeit a much lower peak than in the late 1970s).

- This peak in the late 1990s was followed by declines in use after the turn of the 21st century and an increase in the most recent years.

Trends in Youth Perceptions of Risk

The extent to which young people believe that marijuana or other drugs might cause them harm is an important factor influencing their use of these substances. Lower levels of perceived risk are associated with higher use rates.

Surveys have found some troubling trends in recent years, with young Americans (ages 12 to 17), as the percentage reporting thinking there was a great risk of harm in smoking marijuana has decreased. . . .

These data on marijuana use are of particular concern since trends in the perception of harm of smoking marijuana also have been declining over the same period of time. Prior research indicates that declines in these perceptions are predictive of increases in use. . . .

The Potential Benefits of Taxation

While taxing marijuana could generate some revenues for state and local governments, research suggests that the economic costs associated with use of the drug could far outweigh any benefit gained from an increase in tax revenue.

The existing black market for marijuana will not simply disappear if the drug is legalized and taxed.

In the United States in 2007, illegal drugs cost $193 billion ($209 billion in 2011 dollars) in health care, lost productivity, crime, and other expenditures. Optimistic evaluations of the potential financial savings from legalization and taxation are often flawed, and fail to account for the considerable economic and social costs of drug use and its consequences.

This issue is particularly relevant in the marijuana debate. For example, the California Board of Equalization estimated that $1.4 billion of potential revenue could arise from legalization. This assessment, according to the RAND Corporation, is "based on a series of assumptions that are in some instances subject to tremendous uncertainty and in other cases not valid."

Another recent report from RAND examines this issue in greater detail. The report concludes that legalization and taxation of marijuana would lead to a decrease in the retail price of the drug, likely by more than 80 percent. While this conclusion is subject to a number of uncertainties, including the effect of legalization on production costs and price and the Federal government's response to the state's legalization of a substance that would remain illegal under Federal law, it is fair to say that the price of marijuana would drop significantly. And because drug use is sensitive to price, especially among young people, higher prices help keep use rates relatively low.

The Economic and Social Costs of Legalization

The existing black market for marijuana will not simply disappear if the drug is legalized and taxed. RAND also noted that "there is a tremendous profit motive for the existing black market providers to stay in the market, as they can still cover their costs of production and make a nice profit." Legalizing marijuana would also place a dual burden on the government of regulating a new legal market while continuing to pay for the negative side effects associated with an underground market, whose providers have little economic incentive to disappear.

Legalization means price comes down; the number of users goes up; the underground market adapts; and the revenue gained through a regulated market most likely will not keep pace with the financial and social cost of making this drug more accessible.

Consider the economic realities of other substances. The tax revenue collected from alcohol pales in comparison to the costs associated with it. Federal excise taxes collected on alcohol in 2009 totaled around $9.4 billion; state and local revenues from alcohol taxes totaled approximately $5.9 billion. Taken together ($15.3 billion), this is just over six percent of the nearly $237.8 billion (adjusted for 2009 inflation) in alcohol-related costs from health care, treatment services, lost productivity, and criminal justice.

While many levels of government and communities across the country are facing serious budget challenges, we must find innovative solutions to get us on a path to financial stability—it is clear that the social costs of legalizing marijuana would outweigh any possible tax that could be levied.

Medical Marijuana in Plant Form Should Not Be Legalized

Smart Approaches to Marijuana

Smart Approaches to Marijuana, more commonly known as SAM, is an alliance of organizations and individuals dedicated to a health-first approach to marijuana policy.

Modern science has synthesized the marijuana plant's primary psychoactive ingredient—THC—into a pill form. This pill, dronabinol (or Marinol®, its trade name) is sometimes prescribed for nausea and appetite stimulation. Another drug, Cesamet, mimics chemical structures that naturally occur in the plant.

The Medicinal Value of Marijuana

But when most people think of medical marijuana these days, they don't think of a pill with an isolated component of marijuana, but rather the smoked, vaporized or edible version of the whole marijuana plant. Rather than isolate active ingredients in the plant—as we do with the opium plant when we create morphine, for example—many legalization proponents advocate vehemently for smoked marijuana to be used as a medicine. But the science on smoking any drug is clear: smoking—especially highly-potent whole marijuana—is not a proper delivery method, nor do other delivery methods ensure a reliable dose. And while parts of the marijuana plant have medical value, the Institute of Medicine said in its landmark 1999 report: "Scientific data indicate the potential therapeutic value of cannabinoid drugs . . . smoked marijuana, however, is a crude THC delivery system that also delivers harmful substances . . . and should not be generally recommended. . . ."

It is not so unimaginable to think about other marijuana-based medications that might come to market very soon. Sativex®, an oral mouth spray developed from a blend of two marijuana extracts (one strain is high in THC and the other in CBD, which counteracts THC's psychoactive effect), has already been approved in 10 countries and is in late stages of approval in the U.S. It is clear to anyone following this story that it is possible to develop marijuana-based medications in accordance with modern scientific standards, and many more such legitimate medications are just around the corner.

Recently, the federal government has expanded its enforcement actions against commercialized "medical marijuana" operations. They have closed dispensaries in states, such as California (including the "Harvard" of medical-marijuana learning, the now-defunct "Oaksterdam University"), Colorado and Oregon.

No major medical association has come out in favor of smoked marijuana for widespread medical use.

Marijuana itself is not an approved medicine under the U.S. Food and Drug Administration's (FDA) scientific review process. Yet 16 states and the District of Columbia have permitted marijuana to be sold as "medicine" for various conditions. Although, some of the individual, orally-administered components of the cannabis plant (Marinol and Cesamet are two such drugs available today) have medical value, smoking marijuana is an inefficient and harmful method for delivering the constituent elements that have, or may have, medicinal value. The FDA process for approving medicine remains the only scientific and legally recognized procedure for bringing safe and effective medications to the American public. To date, the FDA has not found smoked marijuana to be either safe or effective medicine for any condition.

In 1997, the White House Office of National Drug Control Policy (ONDCP) requested that the Institute of Medicine (IOM) conduct a review of the scientific evidence regarding the potential health benefits and risks of cannabis and its component cannabinoids. In 1999, the IOM issued the report, "Cannabis and Medicine: Assessing the Science Base," that became the foundation of study into "medical marijuana." For a number of these conditions, the group concluded there would be only limited value in pursuing further research into smoked cannabis because effective treatments were already available. However, they did recommend new controlled studies on cannabis because current research did not provide definitive answers on its risk/benefit profile. The consensus was that in these research studies, smoked cannabis must meet the same standards as other medications in terms of effectiveness and safety. IOM made a series of recommendations pertaining to the use of cannabis in medical treatment that revolve around the need for more research and evaluation. They concluded: "The goal of clinical trials of smoked cannabis would not be to develop cannabis as a licensed drug, but rather, to serve as a first step toward the possible development of nonsmoked rapid-onset cannabinoid delivery systems." And that: "there is little future in smoked marijuana."

The Views of the Medical Community

No major medical association has come out in favor of smoked marijuana for widespread medical use. Further, public health organizations have weighed in:

American Cancer Society: "The ACS is supportive of more research into the benefits of cannabinoids. Better and more effective treatments are needed to overcome the side effects of cancer and its treatment. The ACS does not advocate the use of inhaled marijuana or the legalization of marijuana."

American Society of Addiction Medicine: "ASAM asserts that cannabis, cannabis-based products, and cannabis delivery devices should be subject to the same standards that are applicable to other prescription medications and medical devices and that these products should not be distributed or otherwise provided to patients unless and until such products or devices have received marketing approval from the Food and Drug Administration. ASAM rejects smoking as a means of drug delivery since it is not safe. ASAM rejects a process whereby State and local ballot initiatives approve medicines because these initiatives are being decided by individuals not qualified to make such decisions."

The American Medical Association (AMA) has called for more research on the subject [of medical marijuana], with the caveat that this "should not be viewed as an endorsement of state-based medical cannabis programs."

American Glaucoma Foundation: "Marijuana, or its components administered systematically, cannot be recommended without a long term trial which evaluates the health of the optic nerve," said the editorial. "Although marijuana can lower IOP [intraocular pressure], its side effects and short duration of action, coupled with a lack of evidence that its use alters the course of glaucoma, preclude recommending this drug in any form for the treatment of glaucoma at the present time."

National Multiple Sclerosis Society: "Although it is clear that cannabinoids have potential both for the management of MS symptoms such as pain and spasticity, as well as for neuroprotection, the Society cannot at this time recommend that medical marijuana be made widely available to people with MS for symptom management. This decision was not only based on existing legal barriers to its use but, even more importantly, because studies to date do not demonstrate a clear benefit compared to existing symptomatic therapies and because issues of side effects, systemic effects, and long-term effects are not yet clear."

The American Academy of Pediatrics (AAP) believes that "[a]ny change in the legal status of marijuana, even if limited to adults, could affect the prevalence of use among adolescents." While it supports scientific research on the possible medical use of cannabinoids as opposed to smoked marijuana, it opposes the legalization of marijuana.

The American Medical Association (AMA) has called for more research on the subject, with the caveat that this "should not be viewed as an endorsement of state-based medical cannabis programs, the legalization of marijuana, or that scientific evidence on the therapeutic use of cannabis meets the current standards for a prescription drug product."

John Knight, director of the Center for Adolescent Substance Abuse Research at Children's Hospital Boston, recently wrote: "Marijuana has gotten a free ride of sorts among the general public, who view it as non-addictive and less impairing than other drugs. However, medical science tells a different story."

Since decriminalization passed in 2008, Massachusetts has already seen a rise in youth marijuana use.

Similarly, Christian Thurstone, a board-certified Child and Adolescent Psychiatrist, an Addiction Psychiatrist, and also an Assistant Professor of Psychiatry at the University of Colorado, said:

"In the absence of credible data, this debate is being dominated by bad science and misinformation from people interested in using medical marijuana as a step to legalization for recreational use. Bypassing the FDA's well-established approval process has created a mess that especially affects children and adolescents. Young people, who are clearly being targeted with medical marijuana advertising and diversion, are most vulnerable to developing marijuana addiction and suffering from its lasting effects." . . .

State-Based Medical Marijuana Programs

Major studies by researchers at Columbia University and elsewhere have found that states with "medical" marijuana had marijuana abuse/dependence rates almost twice as high than states without such laws.

Since decriminalization passed in 2008, Massachusetts has already seen a rise in youth marijuana use and now has a 30% higher [rate] than that of the nation.

The Obama Administration has been unambiguous in their opposition to state-based medical marijuana programs and has been routinely raiding state-sanctioned marijuana dispensaries.

For payment of a small cash sum, almost anyone can obtain a physician's "recommendation" to purchase, possess, and use marijuana for alleged medical purposes.

The Department of Justice released two memoranda in 2009 and 2011 stating that that "prosecution of significant traffickers in illegal drugs, including marijuana, remains a core priority" of the Department, and that current policy "was never intended to shield such activities from federal enforcement action and prosecution, *even where those activities purport to comply with state law*. Persons who are in the business of cultivating, selling, or distributing marijuana, and those who knowingly facilitate such activities, are in violation of the Controlled Substances Act, *regardless of state law*."

Studies have shown that in California more than 95% of "medical marijuana" users were not suffering from life threatening illnesses and in one sample of over 4,000 users, 74% of people had used cocaine in their lifetime.

The average user in California was a 32-year old white male with a history of alcohol and substance abuse and no history of life-threatening illness.

In Colorado, according to the Department of Health, only 2% of users reported cancer, and less than 1% reported HIV/AIDS as their reason for marijuana. The vast majority (94%) reported "severe pain."

In Oregon, there are reports that only 10 physicians made the majority of all recommendations for "medical" marijuana, and agitation, seizures, cancer, HIV/AIDS, cachexia, and glaucoma were the last six reasons people utilized marijuana for "medical" purposes.

At present in California, and in several other states, it is widely recognized that the reality of the "medical use" of marijuana is highly questionable. For payment of a small cash sum, almost anyone can obtain a physician's "recommendation" to purchase, possess, and use marijuana for alleged medical purposes. Indeed, numerous studies have shown that most customers of these dispensaries do not suffer from chronic, debilitating conditions such as HIV/AIDS or cancer. Both sides of the argument agree that this system has essentially legalized marijuana for recreational use, at least amongst those individuals able and willing to buy a recommendation. To date many pot dispensaries are mom and pop operations, though some act as multimillion dollar, professional companies. A recent documentary on the Discovery Channel, which examined the practices of Harborside Health Center in Oakland, California—by its own admission, the largest marijuana dispensary "on the planet," the buds (which are distributed directly to member-patients) are merely examined visually and with a microscope. The buds are also handled by employees who do not use gloves or face masks. Steve DeAngelo, Harborside's co-founder, states that they must "take it as it comes." The documentary noted that some plant material is tested by Steep Hill Laboratory, but there was no evidence that Steep Hill's instrumentation and techniques are "validated," that its operators are properly trained and educated, that its reference standards are accurate, and that its results are replicable by other laboratories.

A Petition to Reschedule Marijuana

In the wake of recent enforcement efforts by the Obama Administration, the governors of Washington, Rhode Island, and Colorado have filed a petition with the Drug Enforcement Administration (DEA) to reschedule marijuana. Specifically, the petition asks the DEA to reclassify marijuana from Schedule I to Schedule II of the federal Controlled Substances Act (CSA). The governors contend that such rescheduling will eliminate the conflict between state and federal law and enable states to establish a "regulated and safe system to supply legitimate patients who may need medical cannabis."

> *The mere act of placing herbal marijuana in Schedule II [of the Controlled Substances Act] would not make it available to patients nor address the conflict between state and federal law.*

The current petition takes a unique approach. It seeks to move marijuana to Schedule II "for medicinal purposes only." Marijuana advocacy organizations, such as the Marijuana Policy Project (MPP) and Americans for Safe Access (ASA) are urging other governors around the country to join onto the petition. The petition has garnered considerable publicity, but, as MPP acknowledges, "[r]escheduling is not a cure-all." This is an understatement. Indeed, it is not even a significant step in the direction that the governors, MPP, and ASA hope to move.

Part of the confusion over the actual significance of Schedule II status stems from a misunderstanding of the interrelated, but distinct, functions of the CSA and the Food, Drug, and Cosmetic Act (FDCA). Under the FDCA, the FDA approves *specific medical products* produced by particular "innovator" (for branded products) or generic manufacturers. For example, oxycodone, an opioid, is in Schedule II. Specific products, such as OxyContin® (an extended release form), are also in Schedule II. Physicians prescribe a specific branded or generic product, in a particular dose and dosage form. So until the FDA approves a *smoked marijuana product,* it cannot be prescribed or sold in "dispensaries" for medical use. And the FDA has been clear that smoked marijuana does not pass its rigorous approval standards.

Imagine for a moment that the "medical marijuana" advocates were instead "medical opium" advocates and that various states passed laws decriminalizing (or affirmatively authorizing and regulating) the cultivation and distribution of opium plant material, i.e., opium latex or poppy straw. Even though opium latex and poppy straw *are each in Schedule II,* there would still be a conflict between such state laws and both the CSA and the FDCA. As a well-known drug reform advocacy website states: "If poppies are gown as sources for opiates, there is no question that it violates the CSA." Furthermore, physicians would not be authorized to prescribe, nor pharmacists to dispense, dried opium latex or poppy straw. In order to be prescribed, a specific product containing opiates would have to pass muster in the FDA approval process. Therefore, the mere act of placing herbal marijuana in Schedule II would not make it available to patients nor address the conflict between state and federal law. . . .

Rescheduling is not necessary to make marijuana products available for research. A committee of the California Medical Association recently called for the rescheduling of marijuana "so it can be tested and regulated." However, it is not necessary for marijuana to be rescheduled in order for legitimate research to proceed. Schedule I status does not prevent a product from being tested and researched for potential medical use. Schedule I research certainly does go forward. In a recent pharmaceutical company-sponsored human clinical study investigating a product derived from marijuana extracts, the DEA registered approximately 30 research sites in the U.S. and also registered an importer to bring the product into the U.S. from the U.K., where it was manufactured. And a quick search of NIH-reporter reveals more than $14 million of current research going forward on marijuana and medicine. Research is happening. . . .

The Impact of Medical Marijuana on Drug Use

An in-depth examination of medical marijuana and its relationship to the explosion in use and users came in 2012 from five epidemiological researchers at Columbia University. Using results from several large national surveys, they concluded that: "residents of states with medical marijuana laws had higher odds of marijuana use and marijuana abuse/dependence than residents of states without such laws."

States with medical marijuana laws also show much higher average marijuana use by adolescents, and lower perceptions of risk from use, than non-medical pot states. This would seem to indicate that relaxed community norms about drug use contribute greatly to an increased prevalence of use and users, a situation resulting from the spread of an attitude that "if pot is medicine and is sanctioned by the state, then it must be safe to use by anyone."

Medical marijuana should really only be about bringing relief to the sick and dying, and it should be done in a responsible manner that formulates the active components of the drug in a non-smoked form that delivers a defined dose. However, in most states with medical marijuana laws, it has primarily become a license for the state-sanctioned use of a drug by most anyone who desires it. Developing marijuana-based medications through the FDA process is more likely to ensure that seriously ill patients, who are being supervised by their actual treating physicians, have access to safe and reliable products.

CHAPTER 4

How Should US Drug Policy Be Reformed?

Overview: Public Opinion on Drug Policy

Pew Research Center

The Pew Research Center is a nonpartisan research organization that informs the public about the issues, attitudes, and trends shaping the United States and the world.

The public appears ready for a truce in the long-running war on drugs. A national survey by the Pew Research Center finds that 67% of Americans say that the government should focus more on providing treatment for those who use illegal drugs such as heroin and cocaine. Just 26% think the government's focus should be on prosecuting users of such hard drugs.

A Shift in Attitudes

Support for a treatment-based approach to illegal drug use spans nearly all demographic groups. And while Republicans are less supportive of the treatment option than are Democrats or independents, about half of Republicans (51%) say the government should focus more on treatment than prosecution in dealing with illegal drug users.

As a growing number of states ease penalties for drug possession, the public expresses increasingly positive views of the move away from mandatory sentences for non-violent drug crimes. By nearly two-to-one (63% to 32%), more say it is a good thing than a bad thing that some states have moved away from mandatory sentences for non-violent drug offenders. In 2001, Americans were evenly divided over the move by some states to abandon mandatory drug terms.

"America's New Drug Policy Landscape," Pew Research Center, April 2014, pp. 1–4. (http://www.people-press.org/2014/04/02/americas-new-drug-policy-landscape/). Copyright © 2014 by Pew Research Center. All rights reserved. Reproduced by permission.

The survey by the Pew Research Center, conducted Feb. 14–23 [2014], among 1,821 adults, finds that support for the legalization of marijuana use continues to increase. And fully 75% of the public—including majorities of those who favor and oppose the legal use of marijuana—think that the sale and use of marijuana will eventually be legal nationwide.

By wide margins, the public views marijuana as less harmful than alcohol, both to personal health and to society more generally. Moreover, just as most Americans prefer a less punitive approach to the use of drugs such as heroin and cocaine, an even larger majority (76% of the public)—including 69% of Republicans and 79% of Democrats—think that people convicted of possessing small amounts of marijuana should not have to serve time in jail.

The National Debate About Drug Abuse

The Pew Research Center's report on U.S. drug policy comes at a pivotal moment in the national debate over how best to deal with drug abuse. There is a new bipartisan effort in Congress to give federal judges more discretion in low-level drug cases and reduce mandatory sentences for some drug crimes. Separately, the United States Sentencing Commission is expected to vote soon on a proposal to lessen the federal sentence for drug dealers.

Majorities across nearly all demographic and partisan groups say the use of marijuana should be legal, at least for medicinal use.

More and more states are acting to revise drug laws: Between 2009 and 2013, 40 states took some action to ease their drug laws according to a Pew Research Center analysis of data provided by the National Conference on State Legislatures and the Vera Institute.

The public remains concerned over the problem of drug abuse—both nationally and locally. In fact, a large majority says that drug abuse across the country is either a crisis (32%) or a serious problem (55%). Half regard the problem of drug abuse in their neighborhoods, including its schools, that seriously. These views have not changed much since the mid-1990s.

Public Opinion on Marijuana

At the same time, there has been a major shift in attitudes on whether or not the use of marijuana should be legal. As recently as four years ago, about half (52%) said they thought the use of marijuana should not be legal; 41% said marijuana use should be legal. Today those numbers are roughly reversed—54% favor marijuana legalization while 42% are opposed. . . .

When asked a more detailed question about marijuana use, 44% say it should be legal only for medicinal use, 39% say it should be legal for personal use and just 16% say it should not be legal at all. Majorities across nearly all demographic and partisan groups say the use of marijuana should be legal, at least for medicinal use.

Despite the growing support for marijuana legalization, however, many Americans express concerns over possible consequences from legalization. More than half (54%) say that legalizing marijuana would lead to more underage people trying it. While people 65 and older are most likely to say that legalization would lead to more underage people trying marijuana (69%), roughly half of those in younger age groups—including 51% of those under 30—agree.

On a personal level, most Americans say that, if marijuana were legal, they would be bothered by people using the drug in public (63%), though fewer (41%) would be bothered if a store or business selling marijuana opened in their neighborhood. Just 15% would be bothered if people used marijuana in their own homes.

Have We Lost the War on Drugs?

Gary S. Becker and Kevin M. Murphy

Gary S. Becker was an American economist who died in May 2014, and Kevin M. Murphy is the George J. Stigler Distinguished Service Professor of Economics at the University of Chicago Booth School of Business.

President Richard Nixon declared a "war on drugs" in 1971. The expectation then was that drug trafficking in the United States could be greatly reduced in a short time through federal policing—and yet the war on drugs continues to this day. The cost has been large in terms of lives, money and the well-being of many Americans, especially the poor and less educated. By most accounts, the gains from the war have been modest at best.

The direct monetary cost to American taxpayers of the war on drugs includes spending on police, the court personnel used to try drug users and traffickers, and the guards and other resources spent on imprisoning and punishing those convicted of drug offenses. Total current spending is estimated at over $40 billion a year.

These costs don't include many other harmful effects of the war on drugs that are difficult to quantify. For example, over the past 40 years the fraction of students who have dropped out of American high schools has remained large, at about 25%. Dropout rates are not high for middle-class white children, but they are very high for black and Hispanic children living in poor neighborhoods. Many factors explain the high dropout rates, especially bad schools and weak family support. But another important factor in inner-city neighborhoods is the temptation to drop out of school in order to profit from the drug trade.

The total number of persons incarcerated in state and federal prisons in the U.S. has grown from 330,000 in 1980 to about 1.6 million today. Much of the increase in this population is directly due to the war on drugs and the severe punishment for persons convicted of drug trafficking. About 50% of the inmates in federal prisons and 20% of those in state prisons have been convicted of either selling or using drugs. The many minor drug traffickers and drug users who spend time in jail find fewer opportunities for legal employment after they get out of prison, and they develop better skills at criminal activities.

Mexico offers a well-documented example of some of the costs involved in drug wars.

Prices of illegal drugs are pushed up whenever many drug traffickers are caught and punished harshly. The higher prices they get for drugs help compensate traffickers for the risks of being apprehended. Higher prices can discourage the demand for drugs, but they also enable some traffickers to make a lot of money if they avoid being caught, if they operate on a large enough scale, and if they can reduce competition from other traffickers. This explains why large-scale drug gangs and cartels are so profitable in the U.S., Mexico, Colombia, Brazil and other countries.

The paradox of the war on drugs is that the harder governments push the fight, the higher drug prices become to compensate for the greater risks. That leads to larger profits for traffickers who avoid being punished. This is why larger drug gangs often benefit from a tougher war on drugs, especially if the war mainly targets small-fry dealers and not the major drug gangs. Moreover, to the extent that a more aggressive war on drugs leads dealers to respond with higher levels of violence and corruption, an increase in enforcement can exacerbate the costs imposed on society.

The large profits for drug dealers who avoid being caught and punished encourage them to try to bribe and intimidate police, politicians, the military and anyone else involved in the war against drugs. If police and officials resist bribes and try to enforce antidrug laws, they are threatened with violence and often begin to fear for their lives and those of their families.

Mexico offers a well-documented example of some of the costs involved in drug wars. Probably more than 50,000 people have died since Mexico's antidrug campaign started in 2006. For perspective, about 150,000 deaths would result if the same fraction of Americans were killed. This number of deaths is many magnitudes greater than American losses in the Iraq and Afghanistan wars combined, and is about three times the number of American deaths in the Vietnam War. Many of those killed were innocent civilians and the army personnel, police officers and local government officials involved in the antidrug effort.

There is also considerable bitterness in Mexico over the war because the great majority of the drugs go to the U.S. Drug cartels in Mexico and several other Latin American countries would be far weaker if they were only selling drugs to domestic consumers (Brazilian and Mexican drug gangs also export a lot to Europe).

The main gain from the war on drugs claimed by advocates of continuing the war is a lower incidence of drug use and drug addiction. Basic economics does imply that, under given conditions, higher prices for a good leads to reduced demand for that good. The magnitude of the response depends on the availability of substitutes for the higher priced good. For example, many drug users might find alcohol a good substitute for drugs as drugs become more expensive.

The conclusion that higher prices reduce demand only "under given conditions" is especially important in considering the effects of higher drug prices due to the war on drugs. Making the selling and consumption of drugs illegal not only raises drug prices but also has other important effects. For example, while some consumers are reluctant to buy illegal goods, drugs may be an exception because drug use usually starts while people are teenagers or young adults. A rebellious streak may lead them to use and sell drugs precisely because those activities are illegal.

Usually overlooked in discussions of the effects of the war on drugs is that the illegality of drugs stunts the development of ways to help drug addicts.

More important, some drugs, such as crack or heroin, are highly addictive. Many people addicted to smoking and to drinking alcohol manage to break their addictions when they get married or find good jobs, or as a result of other life-cycle events. They also often get help from groups like Alcoholics Anonymous, or by using patches and "fake" cigarettes that gradually wean them from their addiction to nicotine.

It is generally harder to break an addiction to illegal goods, like drugs. Drug addicts may be leery of going to clinics or to nonprofit "drugs anonymous" groups for help. They fear they will be reported for consuming illegal substances. Since the consumption of illegal drugs must be hidden to avoid arrest and conviction, many drug consumers must alter their lives in order to avoid detection.

Usually overlooked in discussions of the effects of the war on drugs is that the illegality of drugs stunts the development of ways to help drug addicts, such as the drug equivalent of nicotine patches. Thus, though the war on drugs may well have induced lower drug use through higher prices, it has likely also increased the rate of addiction. The illegality of drugs makes it harder for addicts to get help in breaking their addictions. It leads them to associate more with other addicts and less with people who might help them quit.

Most parents who support the war on drugs are mainly concerned about their children becoming addicted to drugs rather than simply becoming occasional or modest drug users. Yet the war on drugs may increase addiction rates, and it may even increase the total number of addicts.

One moderate alternative to the war on drugs is to follow Portugal's lead and decriminalize all drug use while maintaining the illegality of drug trafficking. Decriminalizing drugs implies that persons cannot be criminally punished when they are found to be in possession of small quantities of drugs that could be used for their own consumption. Decriminalization would reduce the bloated U.S. prison population since drug users could no longer be sent to jail. Decriminalization would make it easier for drug addicts to openly seek help from clinics and self-help groups, and it would make companies more likely to develop products and methods that address addiction.

The lower drug prices that would result from full decriminalization may well encourage greater consumption of drugs, but it would also lead to lower addiction rates and perhaps even to fewer drug addicts.

Some evidence is available on the effects of Portugal's decriminalization of drugs, which began in 2001. A study published in 2010 in the *British Journal of Criminology* found that in Portugal since decriminalization, imprisonment on drug-related charges has gone down; drug use among young persons appears to have increased only modestly, if at all; visits to clinics that help with drug addictions and diseases from drug use have increased; and opiate-related deaths have fallen.

Decriminalization of all drugs by the U.S. would be a major positive step away from the war on drugs. In recent years, states have begun to decriminalize marijuana, one of the least addictive and less damaging drugs. Marijuana is now decriminalized in some form in about 20 states, and it is de facto decriminalized in some others as well. If decriminalization of marijuana proves successful, the next step would be to decriminalize other drugs, perhaps starting with amphetamines. Gradually, this might lead to the full decriminalization of all drugs.

Though the decriminalization of drug use would have many benefits, it would not, by itself, reduce many of the costs of the war on drugs, since those involve actions against traffickers. These costs would not be greatly reduced unless selling drugs was also decriminalized. Full decriminalization on both sides of the drug market would lower drug prices, reduce the role of criminals in producing and selling drugs, improve many inner-city neighborhoods, encourage more minority students in the U.S. to finish high school, substantially lessen the drug problems of Mexico and other countries involved in supplying drugs, greatly reduce the number of state and federal prisoners and the harmful effects on drug offenders of spending years in prison, and save the financial resources of government.

The lower drug prices that would result from full decriminalization may well encourage greater consumption of drugs, but it would also lead to lower addiction rates and perhaps even to fewer drug addicts, since heavy drug users would find it easier to quit. Excise taxes on the sale of drugs, similar to those on cigarettes and alcohol, could be used to moderate some, if not most, of any increased drug use caused by the lower prices.

Taxing legal production would eliminate the advantage that violent criminals have in the current marketplace. Just as gangsters were largely driven out of the alcohol market after the end of prohibition, violent drug gangs would be driven out of a decriminalized drug market. Since the major costs of the drug war are the costs of the crime associated with drug trafficking, the costs to society would be greatly reduced even if overall drug consumption increased somewhat.

The decriminalization of both drug use and the drug market won't be attained easily, as there is powerful opposition to each of them. The disastrous effects of the American war on drugs are becoming more apparent, however, not only in the U.S. but beyond its borders. Former Mexican President Felipe Calderon has suggested "market solutions" as one alternative to the problem. Perhaps the combined efforts of leaders in different countries can succeed in making a big enough push toward finally ending this long, enormously destructive policy experiment.

Legalizing Drugs

R.R. Reno

R.R. Reno is editor of First Things, *a journal published by the Institute on Religion and Public Life.*

The weekend edition of the *Wall Street Journal* featured an article advocating the decriminalization of drugs. Economists Gary Becker and Kevin Murphy argue the war on drugs has failed, and social costs of continuing with our current laws are too high. Their solution is to legalize drug use, and eventually the drug market.

The facts seem straightforward. We spend a lot of money trying to prevent drug use ($40 billion they report). Laws against using and selling drugs put very large numbers of men in prison. Like prohibition, criminalization of drugs makes their sale very lucrative—and often dangerous, violent, and destructive of the neighborhoods where business is done. Indeed, whole countries are now convulsed by violence associated with the drug trade.

Given these facts, the argument for legalization isn't stupid. But it's not right.

Consider the analogy to no-fault divorce. Back in the day smart people argued that old divorce laws were unworkable, and that they did more harm then good. There's no fighting social change, we were told, and the punitive divorce laws just make a bad situation worse. Moreover, some argued that existing laws disadvantaged poor people who could not afford to go to Las Vegas for a few weeks to qualify for divorce there, could not pay for lawyers, etc. Better, therefore, to "decriminalize" divorce, as it were. Yes, it might lead to an increase in divorce, but not by much, and in any event the social benefits would far outweigh the negatives.

That's pretty much the way Becker and Murphy argue. They allow that legalization is likely to lead to some increase in drug use, but they assure us that it won't be much. And they even predict that decriminalization will take the stigma out of drug use, which will help people get help to beat addiction to drugs. That's like the argument for no-fault divorce that predicted that taking out the stigma would very likely lead to better outcomes for kids of parents who split up.

I believe we will legalize drugs over the next decades. It fits with the way our meritocracy governs. And I think Becker and Murphy are kidding themselves about the consequences. As has been the case the rest of the cultural revolution of the last fifty years, the meritocrats will use their new freedom wisely, while the weakest and most vulnerable members of society won't. Drug use will join illegitimacy, family instability, and educational dysfunction as problems to be managed and ameliorated.

Easier access to drugs will give upper middle class kids an even greater advantage over all the rest.

Again, the parallel to divorce helps. No-fault divorce became law in many states in the late sixties and early seventies. (It happened quickly, as will legalization of drugs, I think.) During the next decade divorce rates among elites went up. Then they stabilized and went down. Today rich people rarely divorce (the rate is higher than before no-fault, but much lower than most people realize). It's the rest of society that divorces promiscuously.

The same two-America's scenario is the likely long-term result of drug legalization. In fact, it's already the case. My kids went to an inner city high school in Omaha, Nebraska. By their account drinking is widespread, but drug use is almost entirely among the dropouts and non college-bound students. That's partly a function of criminalization, although underage drinking is illegal, which doesn't seem to deter the college bound students. Far more relevant is the fact that drugs are more addictive, more powerful, and more destructive than alcohol. Kids well socialized by upper middle class parents are sensitive to these risks, and for the most part they keep their distance.

Legalization? Easier access to drugs will give upper middle class kids an even greater advantage over all the rest. Like divorce, they'll have the social capital necessary to resist some (but not all) the temptations. The rest? They lack the social capital, and so will be more likely to become victims of the new regime of legal drugs, just as they've become victims of no fault divorce and the sexual revolution more broadly.

Discerning the common good requires more than doing calculations to minimize social costs. It involves passing laws and spending sometimes scarce resources to promote and protect a view of what it means to live an honorable and dignified life. That's why we have laws against drug use, and rightly so. When we get rid of those laws, it will be because we've adopted a different view of the common good, one that is agnostic about what it means to live an honorable and dignified life (even as the meritocrats impose a substantive view on their kids). That's been the trend among secular elites for decades, which is why I think legalization is likely to happen.

Legal, Regulated Heroin
Could Have Saved
Philip Seymour Hoffman

Valerie Vande Panne

Valerie Vande Panne is editor-in-chief of the Metro Times.

A great entertainer overdosed on heroin two weeks ago [February 2, 2014]. He was found dead, a needle hanging from his arm. Dozens of empty drug baggies were found strewn around his apartment.

He was considered a fantastic actor. Influential. Powerful. Insightful. Potent. Everyone, by this time, knows this man's name. It's been plastered across the media landscape not just in the United States, but worldwide: Philip Seymour Hoffman.

The Problem of Drug Overdose

In the days since, there's been all kinds of chatter about the evils of heroin or the need for better drug education. But there hasn't been much talk about the painful, obvious, cold, hard truth: Heroin should be regulated—and not only because science says so, but because, (and again, let's be honest) look around.

Drug prohibition didn't keep us from this great cultural loss. In fact, drug prohibition *causes* thousands of unnamed human losses we suffer day after day, month after month, year after year in this country. Think of the person you know (or your friend who knows someone) who has died because of a heroin, or opiate, overdose. Say their name—because they deserve to be remembered, as much as Hoffman does. And because in a health-centered, rather than law enforcement-centered, world, they didn't have to die.

According to the Centers for Disease Control, "opioid analgesics, such as oxycodone, hydrocodone, and methadone, were involved in about 3 of every 4 pharmaceutical overdose deaths" and "38,329 people died from a drug overdose in the United States in 2010." According to the Office of National Drug Control Policy, from 2006–2010, that was a 21% increase.

Pharmaceutical drugs like Oxycontin are one of the primary reasons we have an opiate addiction crisis in the U.S. in the first place.

Death by heroin increased 45 percent during the same time frame.

The Pharmaceutical-to-Heroin Transition

Allan Clear is executive director of the Harm Reduction Coalition, a non-profit organization that advocates for injection drug users in the United States. When I contacted Clear to comment, he started by reviewing Hoffman's history. "He had problems when he was younger, got help, then he was using pills, then he switched to heroin," Clear noted.

In fact, pharmaceutical drugs like Oxycontin are one of the primary reasons we have an opiate addiction crisis in the U.S. in the first place.

"A fantastic amount of [pharmaceutical] drugs get out there," said Clear. "Cutting back on prescribing can help. Part of the problem is that opiate drugs are out there in too vast quantity. The reason we have a pain pill problem in this country is because of the historic under treatment of pain. Now we have over prescribing."

The pharmaceutical-to-heroin transition is often made when one's opiate prescription ends or is no longer covered by insurance, whether you're rich and famous or poor and on Medicare.

"If we had a maintenance program," Clear continued, "his dependence would've been managed by the medical community, and he wouldn't have needed to graduate to street heroin."

The Maintenance Solution

Maintenance? That's a program where pharmaceutical, clean heroin (or other opiate) is administered in a controlled, clinical setting to addicts who have not benefited from other, more traditional treatments such as methadone.

"The advantage is he can understand what's going into his body and what his dosage should be," said Clear. In addition, "He doesn't have to run out and buy drugs, so it's not a struggle. It takes away anxiety. That kind of constancy and quality control would begin to mitigate some of the adverse reactions to heroin."

The threshold issue is redefining drugs as a health problem. . . . Once that switch is made, then most of the funding has to increase via health and social investments.

In other words, had Hoffman been on heroin or opiate maintenance (if we had such a thing in the United States), it would have been clean, pharmaceutical grade—not cut by unknown drugs—the dose he took would have been known. It might not have killed him, and he would've had medical support throughout the process, so in case of an emergency, he might have been saved.

But many people believe that "there is no safe batch of heroin. It's a killer drug," as Boston mayor Martin J. Walsh recently said. While that is true of street heroin, where the shadowy dealer is in control, it's not true of a pharmaceutical, medical care system of dealing with opiate addiction, such as Clear suggests.

Alex Wodak is President of the Australian Drug Law Reform Foundation. He points to a mountain of evidence that heroin maintenance is cost effective and better for the public health than law enforcement-centered prohibition, calling it "an evidence-based drug policy, rather than the fantasy-based drug policies of the United States."

"The threshold issue is redefining drugs as a health problem," Wodak said. "Once that switch is made, then most of the funding has to increase via health and social investments. Investing money in law enforcement is a waste of time."

Others argue that heroin maintenance does nothing more than use taxpayer money to support, or even encourage, addiction.

The Benefits of a Regulated Drug Market

Thomas Kerr, Associate Professor in the faculty of medicine at the University of British Columbia, has run several NIH [National Institutes of Health]-funded studies of injection drug users. He's also one of the lead scientists evaluating Vancouver's supervised injection facility, Insite. (A supervised injection facility is a place where addicts can take their drug, under the supervision of medical personnel. The site doesn't offer illegal drugs—they simply provide a clean, safe environment, so the person isn't using dirty needles or if they OD [overdose] or want help medical staff is on hand.)

One of the major benefits of a regulated drug market, Kerr said, is "you can be assured of the dose and purity. So many deaths happen as a result of lack of knowledge or purity. Sometimes the heroin can be cut with impurities that make people sick. When people are consuming a drug that is illegal and they are marginalized for their use, they don't know the purity or strength."

By keeping these drugs illegal, and forcing people to turn to an illegal market, "we are causing more harm than the drugs themselves. Imagine every time you wanted to have a drink, you had to go to an unknown source, and every now and then, you got alcohol that contains paint remover. It would burn your esophagus and you'd need to be hospitalized. It seems crazy and makes no sense. But we've tolerated that with drugs like heroin."

There have been numerous heroin trials around the world, including Spain, Switzerland, the Netherlands, Germany, Canada, and England says Kerr, and they show that "when you provide people with pharmaceutical heroin, they can return to work, reduce their involvement in criminal activities, and reduce their illicit use."

Additionally, "We're not talking about a one-off, poorly conducted study. There have been numerous trials conducted in multiple countries with the same results. There is no academic debate about the value of prescribed heroin. It's really a political and ideological debate rooted in an archaic system of drug and law control. That in turn creates stigmatizing and discriminating. The WHO [World Health Organization] agrees this is a health issue."

But others argue that heroin maintenance does nothing more than use taxpayer money to support, or even encourage, addiction. Calvina L. Fay, Director of the Drug Free America Foundation, reports, "Most opiate addicts are polytoxicomaniacs (addicted to several drugs) and [heroin maintenance] programs would supply them with their base drug, free of charge. . . . Psychic effects of opiates make it very difficult to get in touch with the addict emotionally; therefore, psychotherapy is almost impossible. . . . A patient in a heroin maintenance program is still under the influence of the drug and has no motivation to begin a therapy leading to abstinence."

Combatting Addiction with Pharmaceuticals

The United States might seem quite far away from heroin regulation. But there are other tweaks to attitude and policy that can be made.

Coming out of treatment, Clear said people "should be prepared for not only how they remain not using, but they need to be equipped for what to do if they decide to pick up again—Or if someone they come across is."

We have a tightly controlled clinic system that isn't convenient for people. Then we have the criminal sanctions, which leads to secrecy.

This can include making anti-addiction drug buprenorphine available to them, as well as anti-overdose medication naloxone. "In France, they vastly expanded buprenorphine and the overdose rate fell," said Clear. "It's still not as widely used as it could be. Someone who has that history should have that option—and there are not many treatment facilities in the United States that go that route. [It] can be a lifesaver. I've known people who have a history of using, when they know they're going in to a situation [where they might want to use heroin], they take 2–4 milligrams of buprenorphine, to make sure they don't pick up."

In other circumstances, naloxone (also known as Narcan) might work. It's an injectable drug that saves people from dying from heroin overdoses by knocking the opiates off the receptors in the brain—so the person overdosing starts breathing again. (That's frequently how heroin overdoses kill: the person stops breathing.) "It's a weird thing to say," said Clear, "but it is a miracle drug. You have a person who is turning blue and dying, and you give them this drug, and they're breathing again. Suddenly, they're not high. If I were to take it with no opiates in my system, I'd have no adverse reaction to it. It's completely safe." Yet the availability of the drug, which Clear says should be made available to everyone leaving opiate treatment, is patchwork across the country. Some jurisdictions allow family members of addicts to have it. Others permit only the police and EMTs [emergency medical technicians] to carry it. Boston Mayor Walsh just announced all Boston police and EMTs will now carry it after three people died of heroin overdoses in just 48 hours.

It all comes down to "rethinking the way that we utilize medication," said Clear.

There's "also as a protective factor when it comes to overdose. We have a tightly controlled clinic system that isn't convenient for people. Then we have the criminal sanctions, which leads to secrecy. So many people have had their lives destroyed, especially people of color. . . . Those sanctions make it harder to come above ground and seek support, when you don't know what the consequences are."

By removing criminal sanctions and improving access to health-oriented programs, the addicts can stabilize their lives and reduce their involvement in crime.

"There are many scenarios where someone overdoses, and the people they are with leave because they are afraid," Clear continued. "People have been charged with murder for supplying the [injection] that kills them. Just taking the criminal justice system out of it would be a major step forward." Hence, the need for more "good Samaritan" laws that protect people who call for help when someone is overdosing.

Clear also says that the popular idea in the treatment industry—the idea of anonymity, "is a bit of an issue. It would be helpful if people knew how many had these issues, because it makes it less of an issue when so many people have the issue."

Prescription drug Dilaudid, said Clear, (as well as others interviewed for this article), is another solution. An addict could be prescribed Dilaudid without the stigma and resonance that a drug like heroin carries with it.

The Challenges for Public Health Approaches

Many advocates say public health approaches such as these are a big step towards ending the stigmatization of drug users, and say that by removing criminal sanctions and improving access to health-oriented programs, the addicts can stabilize their lives and reduce their involvement in crime.

Others like Fay say that even funding needle-exchange programs is a waste of resources. In Denmark, when there was a heroin maintenance initiative, the opposition to the idea also came from those who had concerns about funding.

And of course not all maintenance programs are created equal, and the opiate addiction drugs we already use regularly, such as methadone, have their problems, too, including being difficult to detox from. Many neighborhoods dislike having methadone clinics in their communities, often because of how the methadone is distributed: the addicts must show up at the clinic every day for their dose, frequently lining up outside, to the disdain of neighbors.

Robert Hämmig, medical director in the addiction department-Bern University clinic for Psychiatry & Psychotherapy, and President of the Swiss Society for Addiction Medicine, said that in Switzerland, the same NIMBY [not-in-my-backyard] problem happens with the heroin clinic there, too, because the addicts cannot take their dose home, so they stay nearby in order to take their dose twice a day, 365 days a year. The most severe side effect some users experience from heroin maintenance is osteoporosis after long-term use. Other than that, says Hämmig, the social side effects of it are related to how it is restricted—such as the lines of people outside the clinic.

Legalization of prescription-based opiate maintenance probably will not eradicate the black market, either.

Still, "It's time for a shift" in policy, said Kerr, especially now that "people realize the system of control and punishment is the worst policy."

Nearly 100 years ago, after all, heroin maintenance was legal in the United States.

Heroin and Rational Choice

Jonah Goldberg

Jonah Goldberg is editor-at-large of National Review Online.

I must say, Kevin's piece today, "Glamour Junkies," is the best thing I've read on drug addiction in a while. As someone who has also known his share of junkies—and other addicts— and who disagrees with Kevin on the wisdom of legalizing heroin, I nonetheless liked the closing quite a bit:

> The model of "rational choice" has taken a beating over the years in the field of economics, and those of us with a broader and less quantitative interest in social questions should take notice. It is hard to develop a rational-choice explanation for junkies unless we consider the very short term, in which case people use heroin for the same reason they use alcohol: They are bored, they are depressed, they are lonely, they cannot sleep, it is a social convention within a certain milieu. And it is associated with a promise, usually unspoken: James Bond's martini is as much a part of his persona as is his Walther PPK and his Aston Martin. A glass of champagne has a certain meaning, a cigarette has a certain meaning, and so does a syringe full of heroin. Those who contemplate the legalization of such substances (and I am one of them) must do so with clear eyes, neither taken in by the romanticism of heroin nor unable to understand how and why that romanticism operates in the culture, and what that means for the choices that people make. It is not the case that no one plans to become a junkie.

I've been something of an outlier on the drug war since I showed up at NR. I've been for decriminalization and eventual legalization of marijuana for years, but for continuing the ban on narcotics like heroin. My reasoning is that pot is like alcohol. It's not great for you, can easily be abused to the point of wrecking your life, but also something responsible people can use in moderation. Moreover, while pot hasn't been around nearly as long as alcohol, it has been around long enough to carve out space in the culture. Society knows how to deal with booze and weed, more or less.

Heroin is different. All recreational drugs make you irrational when high. That's a big reason why people take them—to take a vacation from the ennui, stress, or anguish of sobriety. But drugs like heroin make you irrational when sober too. The more you take them, the more your life becomes organized around taking them. Not everyone who takes heroin once, twice, or even a dozen times becomes a junkie. But each roll of the dice increases your odds, and sometimes it does take just one roll.

Lower the legal heroin age from "never" to 18 and you will see a lot more junkies.

The argument for drug legalization rests on the idea that we are all—more or less—rational actors and that we should be held accountable to our choices. I certainly agree with that as a general proposition. But legalizing heroin will create more irrational actors. Again, not everyone who takes heroin will become enslaved to it. But some will. And if you lower the barriers to obtaining heroin, more will than otherwise would. Yes, personal liberty will be expanded for everyone in theory. But in fact, some people will have given themselves over to a kind of slavery that begins as the mere chemical romance Kevin describes.

I remember early on in my tenure at NATIONAL REVIEW, I asked several of my colleagues whether we would still be against the drug war if we thought the drug war would work. I didn't get a yes or a no in response so much as a "Now, that's a good question!" In other words, the case against the Drug War is not wholly a case for the legalization of drugs. I don't mind passionate opposition to the drug war. I get why it angers so many people. I'm less sympathetic to people who talk about making drug use even more socially acceptable, entirely legal, and vastly more convenient as if that would be great for everybody.

In fairness, I think legalizers make a very plausible argument that, over time, society would figure it all out. We'd set up guardrails on our own, without the help of the State, as the culture absorbed the stupidity of heroin and other hard drugs. But that would take time. Lower the drinking age back to 18 and you will see a lot of drunk teenagers tomorrow. Lower the legal heroin age from "never" to 18 and you will see a lot more junkies. Yes, the next generation might have better foresight from standing on those corpses, but forgive me if I don't see that as a glorious or costless victory for freedom.

As Kevin says, we should look at these things with clear eyes. As a matter of cost-benefit analysis the drug war might not be worth it. But the same sort of cost-benefit analysis would find that surrender would come with a hefty tab as well.

There Is No Moral Justification for the Prohibition of Drugs

Matthew Feeney

Matthew Feeney is a policy analyst at the Cato Institute.

Perhaps in no other policy area are the opinions of lawmakers as different from the opinions of their constituents as drug policy. Despite the fact that more than half of Americans favor the legalization of marijuana, nowhere near fifty percent of policy makers think the same way. This is unfortunate not only because of the degree of human misery inflicted by current policies related to psychoactive substances, but also because the moral arguments in favor of current drug policy are unconvincing and rely on frightening infringements on natural rights.

The Vocabulary of Prohibition

One of the most striking aspects of the drug legalization debate in the U.S. is the vocabulary that is commonly used. It is considered normal for people to discuss the "War on Drugs," despite the fact that these discussions sometimes happen over a beer, a coffee, or amidst a swirl of smoke produced by a nicotine product. Discussions on drug policy also sometimes involve talk of "legalization," when in fact it should more accurately be described as "re-legalization," given that all of the now-banned psychoactive substances at the heart of most drug policy discussions have only been made illegal comparatively recently. The effect of this unfortunate and inaccurate use of language has contributed to making currently prohibited substances seem to many people somehow morally worse than drinking alcohol.

Thankfully, the moral foundations of the prohibition of some drugs are weak. Prohibitionist arguments for banning some drugs because of their effects are inconsistent, and it is impossible for someone to consistently claim to care about human suffering or respect of individual rights while arguing for the continued prohibition of some drugs.

The Consequences of U.S. Drug Policy

Before addressing the moral inconsistencies involved in maintaining a prohibitionist attitude, it is worth outlining the consequences of U.S. drug policy.

Despite the deaths, the mass incarceration, and the financial cost of trying to enforce prohibition the use of illegal drugs in the U.S. has not declined.

Although the U.S. makes up only around 5 percent of the world's population it houses close to 25 percent of the world's prisoners. The U.S. puts more of its citizens behind bars than any other country, with more than one percent of the population serving time behind bars. In federal prisons, inmates serving time for a drug offense make up roughly 50 percent of the population.

U.S. drug policy has had a hugely detrimental effect on minorities. According to the Bureau of Justice, black males were six times more likely to be imprisoned than white males in 2012. According to the most recent data from the Bureau of Justice, almost 40 percent of prisoners are black, despite the fact that African Americans account for less than 15 percent of the American population. The Sentencing Project estimates that one in three black males born recently can expect to go to prison in their lifetime.

The black market, including drug trade, is a fixture of the global economy. Thus, the U.S. drug policy stretches beyond American borders leading to harmful consequences abroad. In the last seven years, more than 70,000 people have been killed in Mexico, thanks in large part to the violence associated to the drug trade. This is much higher than the military and civilian Afghanistan war casualties combined.

Despite the deaths, the mass incarceration, and the financial cost of trying to enforce prohibition the use of illegal drugs in the U.S. has not declined. The so-called "War on Drugs" is a failure.

The Right to Pursue Happiness

In the Declaration of Independence, Thomas Jefferson points out that "Life, Liberty and the pursuit of Happiness" are among our unalienable rights. The English philosopher John Locke said something similar, arguing that people have rights to life, liberty, and property, and that government is obliged to protect these rights. One of the greatest accomplishments of the Founding Fathers was the creation of a state with a political environment that allows for citizens to pursue their own interests, goals, and passions without interference from the state. Under a limited government that protects natural rights the state is limited to ensuring that the rights to life, liberty, pursuit of happiness, and property are protected. Unfortunately, it did not take long for successive administrations to gradually grow the size of the state.

What is not often discussed in drug policy debates is that for many people the use of psychoactive substances contributes to their happiness. Many Americans enjoy consuming alcohol, cocaine, LSD, nicotine, and cannabis precisely because these drugs make them feel a desired effect, be that stimulation, relaxation, or a psychedelic state. What is also often overlooked is that drug prohibition rest on a frightening moral assumption: that the state has the right to criminalize what you do with your most intimate piece of property: your body.

Not only is the desire to consume mind-altering substances thousands of years old, it is also a natural urge and . . . is not unique to humans.

The Desire for Drugs

Taking and using drugs for the purposes of enjoyment is not new to our species. Almost every culture incorporates mind-altering substances somewhere in their myths, cultural practices, or religions. In fact, some have argued that an entheogenic theory of religion should be considered. In his book *Drugged*, Northwestern professor of pharmacology Richard J. Miller discusses the Gobekli Tepe archeological site in Turkey. At Gobekli Tepe, there are 17 feet tall limestone megaliths, some of which are decorated with depictions of animals and insects. Interestingly, Gobekli Tepe has been dated to a time called the "Pre-Pottery Neolithic B Period," meaning that it is older than many ancient sites and predates writing.

However, Gobekli Tepe was not a settlement and seems to have instead been some sort of religious site. Miller considers the possibility that the consumption of hallucinogenic chemicals, which naturally exist in many plants and would have been consumed by our hunter-gatherer ancestors, inspired religion and the building of sites like Gobekli Tepe. Miller quotes Aldous Huxley, who said, "Pharmacology came before agriculture."

Not only is the desire to consume mind-altering substances thousands of years old, it is also a natural urge and, as has been outlined by psychopharmacologist Ronald Siegel, is not unique to humans.

The Exaggerated Harms of Drugs

Despite the prohibitionist rhetoric relating to currently-banned psychoactive substance, the harms and addictive nature of drugs like cocaine, heroin, marijuana, and methamphetamines are exaggerated. Very few people who ever take cocaine or heroin ever become regular users, let alone addicts. In a 2003 article for *Reason*, my colleague Jacob Sullum quoted a Harvard researcher, who said "it seems possible for young people from a number of different backgrounds, family patterns, and educational abilities to use heroin occasionally without becoming addicted."

Columbia University neuropsychopharmacologist Carl Hart has pointed out that methamphetamine, one of the most feared drugs, is "nearly identical" to Adderall and that, "There is no empirical evidence to support the claim that methamphetamine causes one to become physically unattractive."

Prohibitionists need to address the fact that most users of illegal drugs, like most users of legal drugs like alcohol, are not heavy users or addicts. Like people who consume alcohol, most people who use illegal drugs do not do so to excess and are not a danger to society.

Current American drug policy is inhumane, expensive, unworkable, scientifically illiterate, racist, an excuse to grow government, and a violation of our rights.

This is an important point to make in the moral discussions surrounding the legalization of currently-banned drugs because it is sometimes said that prohibitionist polices are justified because legal drugs are somehow less dangerous than illegal drugs. This is nonsense. In order for the current drug policy to be defended, prohibitionists must show why it is morally permissible to pursue happiness by using alcohol but not marijuana.

The Right of Self-Ownership

As well as being an infringement on the right to pursue happiness, drug prohibition also infringes on the right of self-ownership. One of the most terrifying features of the "War on Drugs" is not the human suffering that it inflicts around the world (although this should never be overlooked), but the moral assumption it is built on: the state has the right to control what you do to your body. Even if drugs were as addictive and damaging as prohibitionists say, yielding the right of self-ownership to the state would be worth resisting. If one grants the state the right to control your body it is not hard for the state to justify control over other property.

Although no country has legalized all drugs there are examples of countries that have liberalized their drug laws. Portugal, where all drugs have been decriminalized for over ten years, has not descended into chaos, nor have the rates of use of drugs exploded. The Netherlands also has a far more liberal attitude towards drugs, and has also not become a real-life embodiment of Sodom or Gomorrah. Indeed, in the ten years after drug decriminalization began, drug abuse in Portugal was halved.

Current American drug policy is inhumane, expensive, unworkable, scientifically illiterate, racist, an excuse to grow government, and a violation of our rights. The obvious practical failures of the "War on Drugs" are well known. But it is not often enough said that current drug policy is not only a practical failure, it is a moral one too, and it is almost unspeakably depressing to consider how many lives will be needlessly ruined before enough legislators realize this for America's drug policy to be abandoned.

Drug Legalization Will Have Positive and Negative Consequences

Jeffrey A. Miron

Jeffrey A. Miron is director of undergraduate studies in the department of economics at Harvard University and director of economic policy studies at the Cato Institute.

In December 2013, Uruguay legalized marijuana. Earlier, in 2012, Colorado and Washington legalized marijuana under the laws of their states, and 21 additional states and the District of Columbia have now decriminalized or allowed medical use of marijuana. Portugal decriminalized all drugs in 2001, and the Netherlands has practiced de facto legalization for marijuana for decades. More broadly, many countries have de-escalated their "Wars on Drugs." Indeed, President [Barack] Obama hinted strongly in a recent interview that he supports marijuana legalization.

Legalization advocates, therefore, are feeling optimistic: Many expect full legalization, at least for marijuana, within a few years.

This euphoria is understandable, but premature.

The Harms of Drug Prohibition

Legalizers are correct that prohibition is a terrible approach to balancing the costs of drug abuse against the costs of policies that attempt to reduce drug abuse.

Prohibition drives drug markets underground, thereby generating violence and corruption. Participants in black mar-

Jeffrey A. Miron, "Is the War on Drugs Over?," *The Harvard Crimson*, January 27, 2014.

kets cannot resolve their disputes with courts and lawyers, so they resort to violence instead.

Prohibition makes quality control difficult, so the incidence of accidental poisonings and overdoses is higher than in a legal market. People who purchase alcohol know what purity they are getting; people who purchase cocaine or heroin do not.

Prohibition spreads HIV. Elevated drug prices incentivize injection (users get a big bang for the buck), while fostering restrictions on clean needles. Users therefore share dirty needles, which accounts for a large fraction of new HIV infections in the United States.

Abundant evidence from America's experiment with Prohibition . . . suggests that prohibitions generate only moderate reductions in drug use.

Prohibition harms those who use drugs despite prohibition, since they risk arrest and imprisonment in addition to the negatives of drug use itself.

Prohibition encourages racial profiling and other infringements on civil liberties. Neither party to a drug transaction wants to notify the police, who therefore use more intrusive tactics in the attempt to enforce the law.

Prohibition wastes criminal justice resources and prevents collection of taxes on the production or purchase of drugs, thus adversely impacting government budgets.

And abundant evidence from America's experiment with Prohibition, from state decriminalizations, and medicializiations; from comparisons across countries with weak versus strong prohibition regimes; and from experience with other prohibited commodities suggests that prohibitions generate only moderate reductions in drug use. Some of that reduction, moreover, is a cost of prohibition, not a benefit—since many people consume drugs without ill effects on themselves or others.

Prohibition is therefore a terrible policy, even if one endorses government attempts to reduce drug use. Prohibition has large costs with minimal "benefits" at best in terms of lower use.

Impediments to Drug Legalization

So legalizers are right on the merits, and recent opinion polls show increasing public support for legalization (at least for marijuana). But the negatives of prohibitions have been widely understood at least since the 1933 repeal of alcohol prohibition, yet this has not stopped the U.S. from pushing drug prohibition both at home and abroad.

In addition, further progress toward legalization faces serious impediments.

The first is that recent de-escalation of the Drug War addresses marijuana only. Yet much prohibition-induced harm results from prohibitions of cocaine, heroin, and methamphetamine. Public opinion is less open to legalizing these drugs.

If [legalization] restrictions are so weak that they rarely constrain the legal market, they do little harm. But if these restrictions are serious, they re-create black markets.

Even worse, drug warriors might respond to marijuana legalization by ramping up hysteria toward still-prohibited drugs, increasing prohibition-induced ills in those markets. The public would then observe increased drug-market violence in the wake of marijuana legalization, which would appear to show that legalization causes violence.

A different worry is that while public opinion currently swings toward legalizations, public opinion can change. And marijuana remains illegal under federal law, so a new president could undo President Obama's "hands off" approach.

The Potential Negatives of Legalization

Perhaps the greatest threat to legalization is that many people—including some legalizers—believe policy can eliminate the black market and its negatives while maintaining strict control over legalized drugs. That is why recent legalizations include restrictions on production and purchase amounts, retail locations, exports, sales to tourists, high taxes, and more.

If these restrictions are so weak that they rarely constrain the legal market, they do little harm. But if these restrictions are serious, they re-create black markets.

Legalizers must accept that, under legalization, drug use will be more open and some people will misuse. The incidence of use and abuse might be no higher than now; indeed, outcomes like accidental overdoses should decline. But legalizers should not oversell, since that risks a backlash when negative outcomes occur.

None of this is meant to deny that recent policy changes constitute real progress. But these gains will evaporate unless the case for legalization includes all drugs and is up front about the negatives as well as the positives.

Organizations to Contact

The editors have compiled the following list of organizations concerned with the issues debated in this book. The descriptions are derived from materials provided by the organizations. All have publications or information available for interested readers. The list was compiled on the date of publication of the present volume; names, addresses, phone and fax numbers, and e-mail and Internet addresses may change. Be aware that many organizations take several weeks or longer to respond to inquiries, so allow as much time as possible.

American Civil Liberties Union (ACLU)
125 Broad St., 18th Floor, New York, NY   10004
(212) 549-2500
e-mail: aclu@aclu.org
website: www.aclu.org

The American Civil Liberties Union (ACLU) is a national organization that works to defend Americans' civil rights guaranteed by the US Constitution by providing legal defense, research, and education. The ACLU opposes the criminal prohibition of marijuana and the civil liberties violations that result from it. The ACLU Drug Law Reform Project engages in campaigns and submits briefs in relevant law cases, with literature about these campaigns and text of the briefs available at the ACLU website.

CASAColumbia
633 Third Ave., 19th Floor, New York, NY   10017-6706
(212) 841-5200
website: www.casacolumbia.org

CASAColumbia is a science-based organization focused on developing effective solutions to address the disease of addiction and risky substance use. CASAColumbia is committed to understanding the science of addiction and its implications for health care, public policy, and public education. CASAColumbia publishes reports on the topics of addiction, substance abuse, and legalization, including the report "The Importance of Family Dinners."

Cato Institute

1000 Massachusetts Ave. NW, Washington, DC   20001-5403
(202) 842-0200 • fax: (202) 842-3490
e-mail: cato@cato.org
website: www.cato.org

The Cato Institute is a public policy research foundation dedicated to limiting the control of government and to protecting individual liberty. The Cato Institute strongly favors drug legalization. Cato publishes the *Cato Journal* three times a year and the *Cato Policy Report* bimonthly.

Drug Free America Foundation, Inc. (DFAF)

5999 Central Ave., Suite 301, St. Petersburg, FL   33710
(727) 828-0211 • fax: (727) 828-0212
website: www.dfaf.org

The Drug Free America Foundation, Inc. (DFAF) is a drug prevention and policy organization committed to developing, promoting, and sustaining national and international policies and laws that will reduce illegal drug use and drug addiction. DFAF opposes efforts that would legalize, decriminalize, or promote illicit drugs. DFAF publishes several position statements available at its website, including "Drug Policy."

Drug Policy Alliance (DPA)

131 West 33rd St., 15th Floor, New York, NY   10001
(212) 613-8020 • fax: (212) 613-8021
e-mail: nyc@drugpolicy.org
website: www.drugpolicy.org

The Drug Policy Alliance (DPA) supports alternatives to current drug policy that are grounded in science, compassion, health, and human rights. DPA advances policies that reduce the harms of both drug use and drug prohibition and that seek solutions that promote safety while upholding the sovereignty of individuals over their own minds and bodies. DPA publishes several fact sheets available at its website, including "Moving Away from Drug Courts: Toward a Health-Centered Approach to Drug Use."

Marijuana Policy Project (MPP)

236 Massachusetts Ave. NE, Suite 400, Washington, DC   20002
(202) 462-5747
e-mail: info@mpp.org
website: www.mpp.org

The Marijuana Policy Project (MPP) works to further public policies that remove criminal penalties for marijuana use, with a particular emphasis on making marijuana medically available to seriously ill people who have the approval of their doctors. MPP works to increase public support for marijuana regulation and lobbies for marijuana policy reform at the state and federal levels. MPP works to increase public awareness through speaking engagements, educational seminars, the mass media, and briefing papers, such as "Marijuana Prohibition Facts."

National Institute on Drug Abuse (NIDA)

Office of Science Policy and Communications,
Public Information, and Liaison Branch
6001 Executive Blvd., Room 5213, MSC 9561
Bethesda, MD   20892-9561
(301) 443-1124
website: www.nidanih.gov

The National Institute on Drug Abuse (NIDA) aims to bring the power of science to bear on drug abuse and addiction. NIDA supports and conducts research on drug abuse—including the yearly *Monitoring the Future Survey*—to improve addiction prevention, treatment, and policy efforts. NIDA also publishes the bimonthly *NIDA Notes* newsletter, the periodic *NIDA Capsules* fact sheets, and a catalog of research reports and public education materials, such as "Is Marijuana Medicine?"

National Organization for the Reform of Marijuana Laws (NORML)

1100 H St. NW, Suite 830, Washington, DC   20005
(202) 483-5500 • fax: (202) 483-0057
e-mail: norml@norml.org
website: www.norml.org

The National Organization for the Reform of Marijuana Laws (NORML) works to move public opinion to achieve the repeal of marijuana prohibition so that the responsible use of cannabis by adults is no longer subject to penalty. NORML serves as an informational resource on marijuana-related stories and lobbies state and federal legislators in support of reform legislation. NORML has numerous research and position papers available at its website, including "What the End of Prohibition May Look Like: Preemption and the Legalization of Marijuana."

Office of National Drug Control Policy (ONDCP)

Drug Policy Information Clearinghouse, PO Box 6000
Rockville, MD   20849-6000
(800) 666-3332
website: www.whitehouse.gov/ondcp

The Office of National Drug Control Policy (ONDCP), a component of the Executive Office of the President, establishes policies, priorities, and objectives for the nation's drug control program. ONDCP coordinates drug-control activities and produces the annual National Drug Control Strategy, which outlines administration efforts to reduce illicit drug use, manufacturing, and trafficking; drug-related crime and violence; and drug-related health consequences. ONDCP has numerous publications related to its mission, including the annual *National Survey on Drug Use and Health*, available at its website.

The Partnership for a Drug-Free America

352 Park Ave. S., 9th Floor, New York, NY   10010
(212) 922-1560 • fax: (212) 922-1570

e-mail: webmail@drugfree.org
website: www.drugfree.org

The Partnership for a Drug-Free America is a nonprofit organization that works to help parents prevent, intervene in, or find treatment for drug and alcohol use by their children. The Partnership for a Drug-Free America offers information, tools, and opportunities to connect with other parents and caregivers who may have a child struggling with addiction. The group's website features interactive tools that translate the latest science and research on teen behavior, addiction, and treatment into tips and tools for parents.

RAND Corporation

1776 Main St., Santa Monica, CA   90401-3208
(310) 393-0411 • fax: (310) 393-4818
website: www.rand.org

The RAND Corporation is a nonprofit, nonpartisan research organization that helps improve policy and decision-making through research and analysis. The RAND Corporation's Drug Policy Research Center conducts research to help community leaders and public officials develop better drug policies. The Drug Policy Research Center publishes research, available at its website, including "Marijuana Legalization: What Everyone Needs to Know."

Bibliography

Books

Greg Campbell	*Pot, Inc.: Inside Medical Marijuana, America's Most Outlaw Industry.* New York: Sterling, 2012.
Jonathan P. Caulkins et al.	*Marijuana Legalization: What Everyone Needs to Know.* New York: Oxford University Press, 2012.
Vanda Felbab-Brown	*Shooting Up: Counterinsurgency and the War on Drugs.* Washington, DC: Brookings Institution Press, 2010.
Steve Fox, Paul Armentano, and Mason Tvert	*Marijuana Is Safer: So Why Are We Driving People to Drink?* White River Junction, VT: Chelsea Green Publishing, 2013.
Margaret J. Goldstein	*Legalizing Drugs: Crime Stopper or Social Risk?* Minneapolis, MN: Twenty-First Century Books, 2010.
Erich Goode	*Drugs in American Society.* New York: McGraw-Hill, 2012.
James P. Gray	*Why Our Drug Laws Have Failed and What We Can Do About It: A Judicial Indictment of the War on Drugs.* Philadelphia: Temple University Press, 2012.
David L. Hudson Jr.	*The War on Drugs.* New York: Chelsea House, 2011.

| Michael D. Lyman | *Drugs in Society: Causes, Concepts, and Control,* 6th ed. Boston: Anderson Publishing, 2010. |

Alyson Martin and Nushin Rashidian — *A New Leaf: The End of Cannabis Prohibition.* New York: The New Press, 2014.

Trish Regan — *Joint Ventures: Inside America's Almost Legal Marijuana Industry.* Hoboken, NJ: Wiley, 2011.

Michael J. Reznicek — *Blowing Smoke: Rethinking the War on Drugs Without Prohibition and Rehab.* Lanham, MD: Rowman and Littlefield Publishers, 2011.

Robin Room et al. — *Cannabis Policy: Moving Beyond Stalemate.* New York: Oxford University Press, 2010.

Paul Ruschmann — *Legalizing Marijuana.* New York: Chelsea House, 2011.

Nicholas Schou — *The Weed Runners: Travels with the Outlaw Capitalists of America's Medical Marijuana Trade.* Chicago: Chicago Review Press, 2013.

Katherine Tate, James Lance Taylor, and Mark Q. Sawyer, eds. — *Something's in the Air: Race, Crime, and the Legalization of Marijuana.* New York: Routledge, 2014.

Samuel Walker — *Sense and Nonsense About Crime, Drugs, and Communities,* 7th ed. Belmont, CA: Wadsworth, 2011.

Periodicals and Internet Sources

Doug Bandow   "It's Time to Declare Peace in the
                          War Against Drugs," *Forbes*, October
                          17, 2011.

William J.   "Legalizing Drugs Won't Prevent
Bennett   Abuse," CNN, February 15, 2012.
                          www.cnn.com.

Art Carden   "Let's Be Blunt: It's Time to End the
                          Drug War," *Forbes*, April 19, 2012.

Mona Charen   "Where Ron Paul Is Right," *National
                          Review Online*, December 2, 2011.
                          www.nationalreview.com.

Elizabeth   "Legalizing Drugs Won't Stop
Dickinson   Mexico's Brutal Cartels," *Foreign
                          Policy*, June 22, 2011.

Ralph Espach   "Should Central America Legalize
                          Drugs?," *Atlantic*, February 28, 2012.

Michael Gerson   "Ron Paul's Land of Second-Rate
                          Values," *Washington Post*, May 9,
                          2011.

Marie Gottschalk   "Kicking the Habit," *New Republic*,
                          February 13, 2012.

Glenn Greenwald   "Drug Decriminalization Policy Pays
                          Off," *Politico*, October 14, 2010.
                          www.politico.com.

John Hawkins   "5 Reasons Marijuana Should
                          Remain Illegal," *Townhall*, January 21,
                          2014. www.townhall.com.

Gene Healy — "Pardon Me, but Obama's Right on Clemency for Non-Violent Drug Offenders," *DC Examiner*, April 29, 2014.

Erik Kain — "A Victory Against the War on Drugs," *Mother Jones*, May 31, 2012.

Beau Kilmer — "Has US Gone Further than Netherlands over Marijuana?," CNN, October 18, 2013. www.cnn.com.

Mark Kleiman — "How Not to Make a Hash Out of Cannabis Legalization," *Washington Monthly*, March–May 2014.

Harry Levine — "The Scandal of Racist Marijuana Arrests—and What to Do About It," *Nation*, November 18, 2013.

Sylvia Longmire — "Legalization Won't Kill the Cartels," *New York Times*, June 18, 2011.

Zbigniew Mazurak — "End the War on Drugs Now," *American Thinker*, March 26, 2011. www.americanthinker.com.

Gavin McInnes — "Legalize Pot. It's Bad for You," *Intercollegiate Review*, March 10, 2014. www.intercollegiatereview.com.

John McWhorter — "How the War on Drugs Is Destroying Black America," *Cato's Letter*, vol. 9, no. 1, Winter 2011.

Jeffrey Miron — "Making the Case for Marijuana Legalization," CNBC.com, April 20, 2012. www.cnbc.com.

Ethan Nadelmann   "The Forty-Year Quagmire: An Exit
                    Strategy for the War on Drugs,"
                    Nation, June 17, 2011.

Leonard Pitts Jr.   "If Not Drug Legalization, What, Mr.
                    President?," *Miami Herald*, April 17,
                    2012.

Gustin L.   "A Judge's Plea for Pot," *New York
Reichbach   Times*, May 16, 2012.

Debra J. Saunders   "Medicalization of America's Drug
                    War," *San Francisco Chronicle*, April
                    19, 2012.

Charles D.   "Legalizing Marijuana: Citizens
Stimson   Should Just Say No," *Memorandum*,
                    no. 56, September 13, 2010.
                    www.heritage.org.

Jacob Sullum   "Everything You've Heard About
                    Crack and Meth Is Wrong," *Forbes*,
                    November 4, 2013.

John P. Walters   "Legalized Drugs: Dumber than You
                    May Think," *Weekly Standard*, vol. 17,
                    no. 32, May 7, 2012.

Margaret Wente   "Legalizing Drugs Isn't the Answer,"
                    Globe and Mail (Toronto), October
                    20, 2011.

George F. Will   "Should the US Legalize Hard
                    Drugs?," *Washington Post*, April 11,
                    2012.

Index

T

U

V

W

Y